“We Have a Duty”

Recent Titles in
Contributions in Legal Studies

The Gladsome Light of Jurisprudence: Learning the Law in England and the United States in the 18th and 19th Centuries
Michael H. Hoeflich, editor and compiler

James Madison on the Constitution and the Bill of Rights
Robert J. Morgan

Lawyers, Courts, and Professionalism: The Agenda for Reform
Rudolph J. Gerber

John Marshall's Achievement: Law, Politics, and Constitutional Interpretations
Thomas C. Shevory, editor

Affirmative Action and Principles of Justice
Kathanne W. Green

Unfounded Fears: Myths and Realities of a Constitutional Convention
Paul J. Weber and Barbara Perry

Protecting Constitutional Freedoms: A Role for Federal Courts
Daan Braveman

The Employment Relationship in Anglo-American Law: A Historical Perspective
Marc Linder

The Aristocracy of the Long Robe
J. M. Sosin

Equal Separation: Understanding the Religion Clauses of the First Amendment
Paul J. Weber, editor

Common Law in Southern Africa: Conflict of Laws and Torts Precedents
Peter B Kutner

A History of the Anglo-American Common Law of Contract
Kevin M. Teeven

"WE HAVE A DUTY"

The Supreme Court and the Watergate Tapes Litigation

HOWARD BALL

Contributions in Legal Studies, Number 60
Paul L. Murphy, Series Editor

Greenwood Press
New York · Westport, Connecticut · London

Library of Congress Cataloging-in-Publication Data

Ball, Howard.
"We have a duty" : the Supreme Court and the Watergate tapes litigation / Howard Ball.
p. cm.—(Contributions in legal studies, ISSN 0147-1074 ; no. 60)
Includes bibliographical references.
ISBN 0-313-26565-8 (lib. bdg. : alk. paper)
1. United States—Trials, litigation, etc. 2. Nixon, Richard M. (Richard Milhous), 1913– —Trials, litigation, etc. 3. Watergate Affair, 1972–1974. 4. Executive privilege (Government information)—United States. 5. Separation of powers—United States. I. Title. II. Series.
KF228.U5B345 1990
342.73'044—dc20
[347.30244] 90-3135

British Library Cataloguing in Publication Data is available.

Library of Congress Catalog Card Number: 90-3135
ISBN: 0-313-26565-8
ISSN: 0147-1074

First published in 1990

Greenwood Press, 88 Post Road West, Westport, CT 06881
An imprint of Greenwood Publishing Group, Inc.

Printed in the United States of America

The paper used in this book complies with the Permanent Paper Standard issued by the National Information Standards Organization (Z39.48-1984).

10 9 8 7 6 5 4 3 2 1

For Carol, My Love

Contents

Exhibits

Preface

This book is an effort to examine and analyze the way in which the justices of the U.S. Supreme Court grappled with a political and constitutional issue of enormous proportions that had plagued the national and the international communities for over two years. That issue, of course, was the political and legal events surrounding the abortive break-in (and subsequent cover-up) of the Democratic National Party headquarters in the Watergate Complex in Washington, D.C., in June 1972.

In the recounting of the dramatic tragedy of Watergate from the perspective of the justices, the book uses a number of original sources. These include interviews with some of the brethren, letters from the justices, and, most important, the conference notes and docket sheets of some of the justices, especially Justices William J. Brennan, Jr. and William O. Douglas. Using these materials, along with some other important secondary sources, there is the retelling of the Watergate Tapes litigation story *from the perspective* of the justices who sat and struggled with the litigation at the time.

In order to tell this inside story of the *Nixon* case in a meaningful way, there had to be an examination of the role of the federal judiciary in the political system, an examination of the critically important concept of judicial review, and an examination of the U.S. Supreme Court's processes and personnel at the time of the litigation.

With these foundations in place, the *Nixon* litigation is presented from the inside out. It is an analysis of an institutional opinion from the perspective of most of the brethren (who had to work hard to overcome a number of significant obstacles in order to create it). While it is a detailed examination and analysis of an important controversy that came before the brethren during the 1973 term of the Court, it is also an illustration of the way in which the members of the Court interact in order to resolve conflicts before them.

I want to thank the following persons for providing valuable assistance to me as I pieced together the intricate legal and political strands of the *Nixon* litigation as seen from inside the U.S. Supreme Court.

Hofstra University's annual Conference on the Presidency, sponsored by the University's Cultural Center, enabled me to write an earlier version of the *Nixon* story for presentation at the Conference in the spring of 1988. I appreciate the support and advice offered by the director of that year's program, Professor William Levantrosser, Department of Political Science at Hofstra University.

A panelist on that 1988 program proved to be very helpful. He is Phillip Lacovara, the former special assistant to the Watergate special prosecutor, Leon Jaworski, during 1973–1974. Lacovara provided me with some very important insights into the strategies of the Watergate special prosecutor's team.

Dr. David Wigdore of the Library of Congress has been of great assistance to me and to my assistants as we have pieced the puzzle of Watergate together by pouring over the docket books, conference notes, and other material found in the files of the justices in Washington, D.C.

Two graduate students in Political Science at the University of Utah, Kenny Lawson and Christopher McMahon, provided some critical help to me at various stages of this project and for that I am very appreciative.

My colleague and friend, Philip Cooper, Department of Political Science, SUNY-Albany, has, as usual, given me needed help at the right time.

I also appreciate the various justices of the Supreme Court, and others who had been associated with the Court, who wrote to me as well as spoke to me over the past decade about Watergate and other issues that came before the Court. These include Justices William J. Brennan, Lewis Powell, Harry Blackmun, Byron White, William O. Douglas, Archibald Cox, and (while he was still solicitor general in Edward Levi's Justice Department) Robert Bork.

Dawn Tavares, my secretary at the University of Utah, has also been of invaluable support. She has always responded to my "Dawn, can you do me a little favor" line with a smile and with all the help I needed. I am especially grateful for her question marks on the drafts.

Finally, I wish to acknowledge the loving support of the women in my life: my wife Carol and my daughters Sue, Sheryl, and Melissa.

To these persons, and others, thank you for your help and counsel. I dutifully relieve all of the above of any responsibility for the final product's errors or misinterpretations.

"We Have a Duty"

1

The Supreme Court in the Political System

On Friday, May 31, 1974, the justices of the U.S. Supreme Court met in their traditional secret Conference Session to decide whether to grant an order to set up an expedited hearing in the case of *United States v. Nixon*.[1] Scarcely ten days earlier, John Sirica, the chief judge of the U.S. federal district court in Washington, D.C., had ordered President Richard M. Nixon to surrender sixty-four tapes to the special prosecutor, Leon Jaworski (appointed after the initial prosecutor, Archibald Cox, had been fired by acting Attorney General Robert Bork in the fall of 1973).[2] Mr. Jaworski and his staff were preparing the criminal trial of seven (later six) of Nixon's former White House staff,[3] and it was felt that the presidential tapes would provide important information necessary for the fair administration of criminal justice.

On May 24, 1974, four days after the Sirica order was issued, the president's lawyers filed an appeal in the U.S. Court of Appeals that challenged the constitutionality of the district court ruling. That same day, however, Jaworski took the startling step of seeking Rule 20 review[4] by the U.S Supreme Court before the Court of Appeals decided the questions of law and jurisdiction raised by the president's counsel. The Supreme Court did hear the case in an expedited fashion, after a heated discussion in chambers, and the rest of the legal and political story of the Court's involvement in the Watergate events has become a centerpiece in any account of the Nixon administration's rapid demise after the Court's decision to hold an expedited hearing.

WATERGATE AS METAPHOR AND AS LITIGATION

Watergate has become a metaphor of the age of the Imperial Presidency.[5] Since 1974, millions of persons in and out of public office associate that dramatic event with secret executive department actions that circumvent constitutionality and legality. Whether it is U.S. Marine Corps Col. Oliver North's Iran/Contragate conspiracy trial or some other federal or state official caught in an illegality, the specter of Watergate arises when the deception is uncovered. The event has colored a generation of Americans' views on the basic issue of governmental ethics; Watergate has become a part of the society's political and ethical lexicon.

When government attorneys are asked why they behaved in a duplicitous manner, a basic response is the one offered by a former justice department lawyer. He was involved with the government's World War II forced relocation of Japanese Americans into what one U.S. Supreme Court justice called "concentration camps."[6] He was confronted, in the early 1980s, with evidence (uncovered using the Freedom of Information Act [FOIA]) indicating that the government lawyers for the Justice Department and for the War Department knew that some of the evidence presented against the Japanese Americans was fabricated. He was asked why he and so many other attorneys had so acted. His answer: "Watergate hadn't happened yet."[7]

Watergate is, however, more than the metaphor of an age. It is also a "mischievous decision"[8] by the U.S. Supreme Court that reflected the justices' effort to resolve a specific legal controversy between the U.S. special prosecutor and the president of the United States. The opinion handed down by the Court contained a legal order that led to the resignation of President Nixon a few weeks later. It also contained a controversial judicial interpretation of Article II of the U.S. Constitution with respect to the question of executive privilege.

Watergate was, then, a precedent-setting opinion of the federal judiciary, one that may have lasting impact on the very nature of presidential prerogative long after people have forgotten what happened at the Watergate hotel complex one night in 1972. Although the Court, in a unanimous (8:0) judgment, ordered the president to turn the sixty-four audiotapes over to a federal judge, in the same opinion, the justices expanded the general executive prerogatives of the presidency, by giving a constitutional imprimatur to the concept of executive privilege. A majority of five of the eight justices involved in the Watergate Tapes decision contended that to add to the inherent powers of the presidency was appropriate. (One of the justices appointed by Nixon, William H. Rehnquist, did not formally participate in the *Nixon* discussion, because of his earlier association as deputy U.S. attorney general in the Nixon administration.) Because of the insistence of five justices and a lack of time for the Court to discuss the constitutional issue fully, a faulty precedent was created in 1974.

That the Supreme Court should play a role in such sensational political activity is not surprising to students of American history and politics. While the Court has been from its constitutional beginning an "antidemocratic" institution (in that its members hold what is, effectively, lifetime tenure), it has been involved in the many crises of the Republic, from slavery and economic depression to war and debates over the civil rights of individuals.[9]

THE CONCEPT OF JUDICIAL REVIEW

Expressed in the *Federalist Papers,* Alexander Hamilton's view that the Supreme Court and the federal judiciary constitute the "least dangerous branch" of the new national government is correct in the sense that the federal judges possess neither the power of the purse nor of the sword.[10] However, given their power of judicial review, the justices of the Supreme Court, from almost the beginning of American history,[11] have been able to review critically important cases and controversies and to have their judgments—which possess only the force of moral persuasion—generally accepted by the affected parties in the legal/political dispute. While the Court has no way to actually compel compliance with its rulings, the Court's rulings have been accepted as binding law by the most reluctant of audiences—with only a few notable exceptions.[12]

The concept of judicial review is vitally important to comprehend if one wants to fully understand the essence of federal judicial power in the American political and legal system and, more specifically, the role and function of the justices of the Court in the Nixon tapes political and legal controversy. Judicial review is the power of a court to review an action of a policymaker (using the judge's understanding of the Constitution as the guideline). With the judge following certain codified jurisdictional procedures and established judicial parameters for such review,[13] it is also the power of a court to declare that such governmental action is in conflict with the Constitution and consequently is not valid, or "unconstitutional."

Conceptually, therefore, judicial review is the ability, authority, or power of the judge to declare (in a public opinion) the constitutionality of the actions of a legislature, an executive agency, the chief executive, or an agent of such a public agency. It is the extraordinary power of the judiciary in America (both state and federal) to declare null and void such actions that, in the judge's determination, are in conflict with the Constitution.

A federal court must have the ability to hear a case; that is, it must have jurisdiction over the matter before the judge. Jurisdiction is the threshhold question for the federal judge. "Without jurisdiction the court cannot proceed at all in any cases. Jurisdiction is power to declare the law, and when it ceases to exist, the only function remaining to the court is that of announcing the fact and dismissing the cause."[14] Once the Court notes its jurisdiction over the case, then it may move to the substantive questions raised by the parties to the dispute. In this substantive activity, judicial review can occur.

Although judicial review is not directly mentioned in the Constitution, discussions of such a role for the federal judiciary occurred during the constitutional convention itself. Article III contains the core of this common belief that at some point in the political process, actions of policymakers would be reviewed by the federal judiciary, especially by the justices of the U.S. Supreme Court. The Article states, in part, that "[t]he judicial power shall extend to all Cases, in Law and Equity *arising under* this Constitution, the Laws of the United States, and Treaties made, under their authority" (emphasis added).

There is no doubt that "by 1787, at the onset of the Federal Convention in Philadelphia, the idea of limiting legislative power by judicial nonapplication of statutes in certain cases was clearly understood."[15] During the 1787 Constitutional Convention, the founders rejected the concept of a Council of Revision (consisting of the president and the Supreme Court) that would review the actions of the Congress because of the clearly perceived notion that, in due course, such legislative enactments would naturally come to the attention of the federal courts because they "arise under" the Constitution.[16]

(The opposition to the Constitution came from persons who were concerned about the centralizing powers of the new national government. Some of their sharpest criticisms of the proposed new political system were directed against the Supreme Court. "Brutus," one of the *Antifederalist Papers* authors, sharply attacked the powers of the Supreme Court proposed in the Constitution. For that author, the judges would be "superior" to the elected legislators.[17])

James Madison, reflecting the views of the majority of the Convention's delegates, wrote in his diary that "the Judges ought to be able to expound the law as it should come before them," and that "a law violating the Constitution established by the people themselves would be considered by the Judges as null and void."[18] The voices at the Constitutional Convention took note of the existence of a federal judicial power to review actions of the policy-making branches in order to nullify unconstitutional ones.

It was, however, a cautious Madisonian acceptance of the theory of "judicial paramountcy," as it was labelled by the noted legal scholar Edward S. Corwin.[19] He has argued that Madison, although defending the notion of judicial review, was more comfortable with the concept of legislative supremacy and believed that if the legislature acted in violation of the Constitution's parameters, then the "purely political remedy" was the optimal one. "State 'interposition' to oppose unwarrantable acts of the federal government seems . . . to have been a favorite notion of Madison's."[20]

James Wilson, however, spoke to the notion of judicial review during the ratifying campaign in Pennsylvania when he said, on December 7, 1787, that

> if a law should be made inconsistent with those powers vested by this instrument in Congress, the judges, as a consequence of their independence, and the particular powers to government being defined, will declare such law to be null and void; for the power of the Constitution predominates. Anything, therefore, that shall be enacted by Congress contrary thereto, will not have the force of law.[21]

Therefore, while Chief Justice John Marshall crystallized and justified the Court's power of judicial review for the Supreme Court in 1803, it was but a formalization of a concept that had been generally accepted by Americans for generations. *Marbury* revealed both colonial and constitutional precedents and attitudes.[22] It followed, too, a number of earlier Supreme Court decisions in which the Court had exercised its power of judicial review over federal statutes while upholding their legitimacy as being consistent with the fundamental law.[23] While the Court in 1797 set aside a Virginia statute,[24] *Marbury* was the first instance of the Supreme Court actually voiding an action of the Congress.

From these constitutional era beginnings, the concept of judicial review has had a long, often controversial history. Some, including judges,[25] have critically commented that judicial review "is fundamentally inconsistent with the theory of electorally accountable government."[26] Nixon's brief presented to the Court in June 1974 took a similar tack. According to his counsel, "the only constitutional recourse against a President is by impeachment and through the electoral process."[27] Much like Judge Gibson and Associate Justice Frankfurter, Nixon argued against the implementation of judicial review by the Supreme

Court in the extremely politicized case of *U.S. v. Nixon*. For the president, the Watergate Tapes case was as much of a nonjusticiable "political question" as was the malapportionment issue. In any discussion of judicial review, therefore, it is appropriate to review the limits of that concept.

THE LIMITS OF JUDICIAL REVIEW

While judicial review is a basic tool of the federal judges, it is not used indiscriminately by them. As a noted scholar once wrote: "Judicial self-restraint and judicial power seem to be the opposite sides of the same coin; it has been by judicious application of the former that the latter has been maintained. . . . The Court's power has been maintained by a wise refusal to employ it in unequal combat."[28] Over the generations, the federal judiciary, primarily the U.S. Supreme Court, have created and regularly applied what Alexander Bickel referred to as a set of "passive virtues"[29] in order to avoid the unnecessary confrontation with other governmental agencies. As Justice John M. Harlan II once observed, dissenting in *Baker v. Carr*, federal courts were not "the last refuge for the correction of all inequality or injustice, no matter what its nature or its source."[30] As will be seen, this view was a minority view during the Warren Court years.

These passive virtues, developed as procedural instruments by Court majorities in actual cases and controversies heard by the brethren, serve as gatekeeping devices. Controlling the extent of the federal judiciary's jurisdictional door's opening determines the kinds of cases the federal judges hear. The federal judges, in total control of the door to the courthouse, want to "make sure they do not handle controversies that the[y] feel it imprudent to handle."[31]

U.S. Supreme Court majorities for over two hundred years have fashioned these rules for the federal judiciary. In so doing, they limit the inherent power of judicial review. Although the federal judges, including the justices of the U.S. Supreme Court, cannot use the Article III[32] judicial powers until a case or controversy comes along, they will not use their power of judicial review if they believe that a dispute brought before them does not merit judicial examination.

When the federal judges raise such "threshold" questions, they are determining "whether a person's dispute with another party is deserving of judicial resolution."[33] These judicially created gatekeeping tools include the following doctrines or concepts: standing to sue, the case and controversy doctrine, ripeness and mootness, the *nonjusticiable* "political question" doctrine and the parsimonious *Ashwander*[34] rules.

A person who initiates litigation in a federal court must be an actual, concrete party to the dispute. If there is concreteness present, the party is said to have *standing to sue.* Absent that direct linkage with injury of some sort, there is no standing, no constitutionally derived case or controversy, and the litigation cannot be heard in the federal courthouse. The case of controversy rule means that there must be actual controversy between the parties to a dispute; unlike some state courts, due to the language of the Constitution, the federal judiciary cannot hand down an advisory opinion. A third party who has not suffered a direct injury cannot bring suit in a federal court.[35] Also, the direct, concrete injury must be one that is legally protected by statute or constitution.

Ripeness and mootness are two sides of a coin. Ripeness means that a suit must be brought to the federal court at the proper, that is, ripe, time. Mootness is the situation where parties to a proper suit at the start of the litigation proceedings no longer are in an adversarial situation and are no longer considered injured parties. Courts do not sit to "decide arguments after events have put them to rest."[36]

Assuming jurisdiction and standing, there is another threshold concept that has been developed and used by the federal judges for over a century. This is the concept of *justiciability.* A case is said to be *justiciable* if the justices of the Court believe the case is capable of judicial resolution. Clearly, this judicial judgment is a subjective assessment. As Chief Justice Earl Warren said: "Justiciability is itself a concept of uncertain meaning and scope. . . . Justiciability is not a legal concept with a fixed content or susceptible of scientific verification. Its utilization is the resultant of many subtle pressures."[37]

A most interesting use of the justiciability idea has been the Supreme Court's creation of the "political question" doctrine. This concept, when applied, turns a jurisdictional issue into a *nonjusticiable* one, that is, the federal judges have decided that the issue is incapable of judicial resolution, and therefore it is a "political question" that falls outside the scope of judicial intervention. Typically, those questions that the federal judge thinks are better resolved in the political process, rather than in the Court, are labelled nonjusticiable "political questions." As the Court majority would say in such a setting, it is appropriate for the federal court to stay out of the "political thickets."[38]

For example, for the longest time, the president's ability to conduct foreign affairs or the power to wage war or, to take another example, the legislature's responsibility to raise funds to support the war effort, were considered "political questions" by the federal judiciary. However, this concept, like all the rest, is accordian-like and subject to redefinition by another Court led by a different type of chief.

A recent example of the "political question" doctrine's flexibility involved the president and the Senate. In June 1979, a group of national legislators brought a suit in federal district court challenging the unilateral termination of the Mutual Defense Treaty of 1954 with the Republic of China (Taiwan) by President Jimmy Carter in December 1978. While a federal district court judge acknowledged that Senator Barry Goldwater (R-AZ) and others had suffered derivative injury, that is, an injury based on the right to exercise the powers of the legislature and ruled substantively on the merits of the claim,[39] the Supreme Court majority, in a summary judgment, determined that the matter was a nonjusticiable political question. In a brief *per curiam* order, the Court vacated the judgment of the U.S. Court of Appeals and remanded the case back to the district court with direction to Judge Gasch to dismiss the complaint.

Attached to the short order were four opinions written by the brethren. Rehnquist, joined by Stewart, Burger and Stevens, concluded that it was a political question.[40] Powell's concurring opinion supported the action because there was no standing to sue because of a lack of ripeness. In dicta, he stated that the case posed no political question, and courts should hear such cases when standing is present.[41] Blackmun, joined by White, dissented because he believed that the case should have been scheduled for briefs on the merits and oral argument. Brennan dissented because, in his view, the case had standing, was not a political question, and the president had the power to unilaterally terminate a treaty. For Brennan, the Rehnquist opinion "profoundly misapprehends the political question principle as it applies to matters of foreign relations. . . . The issue . . . falls within the competency of the courts."[42]

A final class of passive virtues are a number of self-imposed judicial guidelines created in a case heard in the 1930s that are still referred to by federal judges when they decline to take a case on the merits. In a 1936 concurrence, Justice Louis Brandeis listed some classic rules of judicial parsimony, rules that have become known as the *Ashwander* rules. Basically, these rules suggested ways that the Court could avoid clashes with the coordinate branches of the national government. Essentially, these parameters of restraint encourage the federal judge to assiduously avoid constitutional interpretation in a case or controversy when the jurist could dispose of the conflict on less formidible grounds such as statutory construction.

THE WARREN COURT'S HERITAGE: A MORE EXPANSIVE USE OF JUDICIAL REVIEW

The use of judicial review by the federal courts has been discussed by the federal judges themselves, by the legal community, by the political agents, and by the public ever since *Marbury v. Madison* (1803). During the era of the "Super Chief's" Court, that is, Earl Warren and his active, liberal majority,[43] the Court majority was less cautious about employing the passive virtues. The Warren Court majority acted on the belief that there were occasions when "judicial displacement of legislative [and other] decisions [was] justified," and they rejected the contrary principle that stated that "judges cannot justifiably do whatever they want, but must respect some constraints on their behavior as judges."[44]

As a result of such "incaution" (beginning with the watershed *Brown v. Board of Education* opinion in May 1954), according to Abram Chayes, the Warren Court brought about a major change in federal judicial behavior. Federal courts have begun to "deal with grievances over the administration of some public or quasi-public program and to vindicate the public policies embodied in the governing statutes or constitutional provisions. As a result, courts are inevitably cast in an affirmative, political—activist, if you must—role. Whether they realized it or not, [the Warren Court justices] had committed the federal courts to an enterprise of profound social reconstruction."[45]

With the announcement of *Brown* in 1954, the Supreme Court, under Chief Justice Warren's growing, assertive leadership, "reasserted itself as an independent force in American politics and ended nearly two decades of relative docility in the wake of the New Deal crisis."[46] Since then, the Court has become heavily involved in criminal justice issues (the "incorporation" of most of the procedural rights in the Bill of Rights into the "due process" language of the Fourteenth Amendment), as well as issues such as school prayer, reapportionment, busing, privacy, abortion, and voting rights. Furthermore, the lower federal court judiciary, especially the district court judges, have become much more involved in the resolution of political and social problems.[47]

Although a number of the Warren Court brethren were no longer on the Court in 1973, there still remained an active, noninterpretivist[48] core of activist brethren. Among them were William J. Brennan, Thurgood Marshall, and William O. Douglas. These three men were defenders of a conception of judicial review that maintained that federal judges were "authorized, if not duty-bound, to protect individuals against governmental interference with these [personal] rights, which can be discovered in conventional morality or derived through the methods of philosophy and adjudication."[49]

(After Watergate, the most outspoken jurist on the contemporary Supreme Court on behalf of this noninterpretivist position has been Associate Justice William J. Brennan, Jr. During the mid-1980s, for example, he engaged in a public debate of sorts on this question of interpretivist versus noninterpretivist judicial review with Edwin Meese II, President Ronald Reagan's very controversial attorney general.[50])

In the 1973–1974 Watergate litigation, the president's attorneys vigorously argued that the federal courts did not have the jurisdiction, that is, the constitutional authority, to hear that particular case. While they did not argue that the federal courts lacked the constitutional power to hear cases involving presidential actions, they did strenuously maintain that the application of judicial review by the federal courts in this instance violated the principle of separation of powers. Although they claimed to have accepted the power of judicial review, they argued that another equally potent principle of constitutional government, the separation of powers, made the case nonjusticiable, and therefore the Court did not have the power to hear the case.

It fell to the justices of the Supreme Court, however, as it always does, to decide whether there was merit to that legal argument. The Court rejected the jurisdictional claim, ruled on the merits, and in so acting led to the resultant incongruity: the resignation of a sitting president while strengthening the inherent powers of the presidency.

This book reexamines, through an analysis of the justices' papers (especially those of William J. Brennan, Jr. and William O. Douglas), the shared behaviors of the judges in reaching their decision in the controversial case of *United States v. Nixon*. If, as Justice Potter Stewart once said, the "business of the Court is to give institutional opinions for its decisions,"[51] this opinion of the Court, a unanimous one, "provides a good . . . example of the justices working toward an institutional decision and opinion."[52]

In addition, tracing the creation of the opinion in *United States v. Nixon* on the basis of documents illuminating the judicial goings-on inside the Court's Marble Palace enables one to understand the dynamics of Supreme Court decision making. Understanding the Court and its potent power of judicial review through an examination of the *Nixon* litigation also illuminates the axiom that Associate Justice Robert Jackson postulated about the Supreme Court. "We are not final because we are infallible," he wrote in a concurring opinion, "but we are infallible only because we are final."[53]

NOTES

1. *United States v. Nixon,* 418 *U.S.* 683 (1974). This litigation arose as a consequence of litigation in federal court, *Nixon v. Sirica,* in the fall of 1973. In the earlier case, the first special prosecutor, Archibald Cox, had asked that the president, in accordance with a subpoena, turn over six tapes that were needed, it was alleged, for review by the Grand Jury that was then sitting. Cox had argued, and the federal court had agreed, that the tapes were "material and important evidence." Nixon countered with the soon-to-be-routine response that "the President is not subject to compulsory process from the courts. The independence of our three branches of government is at the very heart of our constitutional system. It would be wholly inadmissible for the Court to seek to compel some particular action from the President." In his order, Sirica dismissed the contention that there was a constitutionally based executive privilege and rejected the argument that it was the president who "finally determines whether its privilege is properly invoked . . . [for] that is a judicial decision. Judicial control over the evidence in a case cannot be abdicated to the caprice of executive officers." On October 12, 1973, The U.S. Court of Appeals, D.C. Circuit, in a five person *per curiam* opinion with two dissents, upheld Sirica's order to the president (to turn the tapes over to the federal judge for an *in camera* inspection and determination of usefulness to the special prosecutor.) The federal appeals court concluded that Nixon had "no justification, on confidentiality grounds, for depriving the grand jury of the best evidence of the conversations available." The president, the majority noted, "is not above the law's commands. . . . Incumbency does not relieve the President of the routine legal obligations that confine all citizens." With some of the tapes finally turned over to Sirica and then to the new special prosecutor, Leon Jaworski, the Grand Jury proceeded to indict a number of individuals. At that point, Jaworski sought, through the subpoena process, additional tapes held by the president for use in the upcoming (September 1974) trial of the persons indicted.

2. Bork's actions in the "Saturday Night Massacre" were reviewed when Bork was nominated for a seat on the U.S. Supreme Court (to replace Associate Justice Lewis F. Powell, who had resigned in June 1987) in July 1987 by President Ronald Reagan. Bork recounted, in his

testimony before the Senate Judiciary Committee, that both Elliot Richardson and William Ruckelshous had suggested that Bork not resign in order to provide continuity to a battered Justice Department as well as to make sure that the special prosecutor's staff continued its work. See U.S. Senate, Report of the Committee on the Judiciary, *Nomination of Robert H. Bork to Be an Associate Justice of the U.S. Supreme Court*. 100th Congress, 1st Session (1987), p. 295.

3. The seven included John Mitchell, John D. Ehrlichman, H.R. Haldeman, Gordon Strachan, Robert Mardian, Kenneth Parkinson, and Charles Colson. Colson was later removed from the proceedings when on June 3, 1974, he pleaded guilty to the charge of obstruction of justice.

4. Rule 20 of the Supreme Court Rules of Procedures states that the Supreme Court can grant a writ of certiorari to "review a pending case in a court of appeals, before judgment is given in such court" if the justices are convinced that the case "is of such imperative public importance as to justify the deviation from normal appellate processes and to require immediate settlement" in the Court.

5. Arthur M. Schlesinger, Jr., *The Imperial Presidency* (Boston: Houghton Mifflin, 1973).

6. Justice Owen Roberts dissenting, *Korematsu v. United States*, 323 *U.S.* 214 (1944).

7. See Peter Irons, *Justice At War* (New York: Oxford University Press, 1985).

8. Phillip Lacovara interview, November 21, 1987, Hofstra University, Hempstead, N.Y.

9. Throughout the history of the Republic, from *Dred Scott v. Sanford* 60 *U.S.* 393 (1857) and *Plessy v. Ferguson* 163 *U.S.* 537 (1896) to *Brown v. Board of Education* 347 *U.S.* 483 (1954) and *Alexander v. Holmes County, Mississippi* 396 *U.S.* 1218 (1969)—race relations, from *Lochner v. New York* 198 *U.S.* 45 (1905) to *West Coast Hotel Co. v. Parrish* 300 *U.S.* 379 (1937)—economic regulations, from *Luther v. Borden* 7 *Howard* 1 (1849) and *Colegrove v. Green* 328 *U.S.* 549 (1946) to *Baker v. Carr* 369 *U.S.* 186 (1962) and *Reynolds v. Sims* 377 *U.S.* 533 (1964)—political questions/republican government, from *Schenck v. United States* 249 *U.S.* 47 (1918) to *New York Times v. United States* 403 *U.S.* 713 (1971)—First Amendment, the justices of the Court have been involved in the affairs of the nation.

10.

> The judiciary . . . will always be the least dangerous to the political rights of the Constitution. . . . The Courts were designed to be an intermediate body between the people and the legislature, in order, among other things, to keep

the latter within the limits assigned to their authority. The interpretation of the laws is the proper and peculiar province of the courts. A constitution is, in fact, and must be regarded by the judges, as a fundamental law. It therefore belongs to them to ascertain its meaning, as well as the meaning of any particular act proceeding from the legislative body. If there should happen to be an irreconcilable variance between the two, that which has the superior obligation and validity ought, of course, to be preferred; or, in other words, the Constitution ought to be preferred to the statute, the intention of the people to the intention of their agents.

James Madison, Alexander Hamilton, John Jay, *The Federalist Papers*, ed. Isaac Kramnick (New York: Penguin Books, Ltd., 1987), 78, 81, pp. 436–41, 450–58, *passim*.

11. *Marbury v. Madison* 1 Cranch 137 (1803).

12. See, for example, Ellis Katz, "Patterns of Compliance with the Schempp Decision," *Journal of Public Law* 14 (1965): 396–408, and Stephen L. Wasby, *The Impact of the United States Supreme Court* (Homewood, IL: Dorsey Press, 1970).

13. There must be a concrete case or controversy before the Court, as defined in the Constitution, the U.S. Code, and as defined by the Court itself in its own case law on the matter of standing to sue, mootness, "political question," and on the general question of jurisdiction itself.

14. *Ex Parte McCardle*, 74 *U.S.* 506 (1869).

15. Robert Lowry Clinton, *Marbury v. Madison and Judicial Review* (Lawrence, KS: University Press of Kansas, 1989), p. 56. Clinton noted that limitation "had been accomplished in America by Courts operating under both written and unwritten 'constitutions' in the colonial and revolutionary periods. These were not merely isolated occurrences, but may be viewed as normal extensions of English rules and practices, applied in the American context." Ibid.

16. Luther Martin, a representative from Maryland, said (in opposing the Supreme Court's participation in the proposed Council of Revision) that "as to the constitutionality of laws, that point will come before the judges in their official character. In this character they have a negative on the laws. Join them with the executive on the [Council of R]evision, and they will have a double negative." Quoted in Winton U. Solberg, ed., *The Federal Convention and the Formation of the Union of the American States* (Indianapolis: Bobbs-Merrill, 1958), pp. 238–39.

17. Wrote Brutus: "The judges in England are under the control of the legislature, for they are bound to determine according to the laws passed by them. But the judges under this Constitution will control the legislature, for the supreme court are authorized in the last resort, to determine what is the extent of the powers of the Congress. They

are to give the constitution an explanation, and there is no power above them to set aside their judgment." *New York Journal*, March 20, 1788, Ralph Ketcham, ed., *The Anti-Federalist Papers of the Constitutional Convention Debate* (New York: New American Library, 1986), pp. 304–5.

18. Solberg, *Federal Convention*, p. 98. Elbridge Gerry's statement, recorded by Madison, concluded that the judges would thus be "free from the bias of having participated in [the law's] formation."

19. See Edward S. Corwin, "Supreme Court and Unconstitutional Acts of Congress," *Michigan Law Review* 4, no.616 (1906).

20. Ibid. In testimony before a congressional committee (Senate Judiciary) that was examining President Roosevelt's 1937 "Court Packing" Plan, Corwin clashed with one of the members of the Committee, Senator King. The legislator had pointed out that Corwin's views on the issue of delegate acceptance of judicial review at the 1787 convention were in the minority and that there were over thirty five of the delegates, including Madison, who supported judicial review in the summer of 1787. See "Reorganization of the Federal Judiciary," U.S. Congress, Senate, Committee on the Judiciary, 75th Congress, First Session, 1937, reprinted in Richard Loss, ed., *Corwin on the Constitution* (Ithaca: Cornell University Press, 1987), pp. 218–277.

21. Solberg, *Federal Convention*, p. 178. It is quite clear that "the convention exhibited a near-unanimous agreement on the necessity for placing external limitations on the power of Congress." Clinton, *Marbury*, p. 60.

22. Colonial precedents include arguments against the Writs of Assistance (1761) as well as Massachusetts, Virginia, New York, Rhode Island, and North Carolina Court actions that employed judicial review to strike down political enactments. See, generally, Clinton, *Marbury v. Madison, passim.*

23. See, for example, *Hayburn's Case* 2 *Dall* 409 (1792), *Van Horne's Lessee v. Dorrance* 2 *Dall* 304 (1795), and *Hylton v. United States*, 3 *Dall* 171 (1796).

24. "It is, indeed, a general opinion [and] is expressly admitted by all at this bar, and some of the Judges have, individually, in the circuits, decided, that the Supreme Court can declare an Act of Congress to be unconstitutional, and therefore, is invalid; but there is no adjudiciation of the Supreme Court itself of this point." *Cooper v. Telfair* 4 *Dall* 14 (1800).

25. See, for example, Judge Gibson dissenting in *Eakin v. Raub*, 12 *S and L* 330 (1825): "It rests with the people [not the Court] in whom full and absolute sovereign power resides, to correct abuses in legislation by instructing their representatives to repeal the obnoxious act."

In his dissent in *Baker v. Carr*, 369 *U.S.* 186 (1962), Justice Felix Frankfurter (joined by Justice Harlan) wrote that changes must come, not from a Court using judicial review, but from "an informed, civically militant electorate [with] an aroused popular conscience that sears the conscience of the people's representatives."

26. Earl M. Maltz, "Murder in the Cathedral: The Supreme Court as Moral Prophet," *University of Toledo Law Review* 8, no.3 (Summer 1983), at 631.

27. Brief reprinted in Alan Westin and Leon Friedman, eds., *United States v. Nixon* (New York: Chelsea House, 1974), p. 324.

28. John P. Roche, "Judicial Self-Restraint," *American Political Science Review*, 49, no.722 (September 1955).

29. Alexander M. Bickel, *The Least Dangerous Branch: The Supreme Court at the Bar of Politics* (New York: Bobbs-Merrill, 1962), pp. 111 ff.

30. Harlan, dissenting, *Baker v. Carr*, 369 *U.S.* 186 (1962).

31. Walter F. Murphy and C. H. Pritchett, *Courts, Judges and Politics* (New York: Random House, 1975), p. 75.

32. Article III enumerates the judicial power of the federal judiciary. These powers, both original and appellate, extend to all cases and controversies arising under the Constitution. It states:

"The judicial power shall extend to all cases, in law and equity, arising under this constitution, the laws of the United States, and treaties made, or which shall be made, under their authority; to all cases affecting ambassadors, other public ministers and consuls; to all cases of admiralty and maritime jurisdiction; to controversies to which the United States shall be a party; to controversies between two or more states, between a state and citizens of another state (See Amendment 11), between citizens of different states, between citizens of the same state claiming lands under grants of different states, and between a state, or the citizens thereof, and foreign states, citizens or subjects. In all cases affecting ambassadors, other public ministers and consuls, and those in which a state shall be party, the supreme court shall have original jurisdiction. In all the other cases before mentioned, the supreme court shall have appellate jurisdiction, both as to law and fact, with such exceptions, and under such regulations as the Congress shall make."

33. David W. Rohde and Harold J. Spaeth, *Supreme Court Decision Making* (San Francisco: Freeman, 1976), p. 13.

34. *Ashwander v. Tennessee Valley Authority*, 297 *U.S.* 298 (1936).

35. *Tileston v. Ullman*, 318 *U.S.* 44 (1943).

36. Wallace Mendelson, "Mr. Justice Douglas and Government by Judiciary," *Journal of Politics* 38, no.4 (November 1976): 937.

37. *Flast v. Cohen*, 392 *U.S.* 83 (1968).

38. See, for example, Felix Frankfurter's opinion in the 1946 reapportionment case of *Colegrove v. Green* 328 *U.S.* 549 (1946). Reappor-

tionment was a classic example of a nonjusticiable political question until another Court majority, led by the "Super Chief," Earl Warren, announced in 1962 (*Baker v. Carr*, 369 *U.S.* 186) that reapportionment was a justiciable issue and that there were numerous Fourteenth Amendment Equal Protection remedies to rectify the wrongs brought on by malapportioned legislatures. In dissent, Frankfurter argued that judicial entanglement in political thickets will destroy the image of the federal court as one of "complete detachment from political entanglements." See, generally, Howard Ball, *The Warren Court's Conceptions of Democracy* (Rutherford, New Jersey: Fairleigh Dickinson University Press, 1971).

39. Judge Oliver Gasch ruled that the Constitution commanded mutual action by the president and Congress by having Carter submit the termination to the Senate for its advice and consent. The president, he concluded, was not "the sole maker of foreign policy." The federal court of appeals, sitting *en banc*, overturned Gasch on the merits. Two judges concurred in the result but argued that there was no standing to sue. See *Goldwater v. Carter*, No.78-2412, USDC, *Memorandum Order*, Gasch, O, Judge; *Goldwater v. Carter*, CA/DC, 48 Law Week, 2388-2389 (1979).

40. "The basic question is 'political' and therefore nonjusticiable because it involves the authority of the President's conduct of our nation's foreign policy and the extent to which the Senate or the Congress is authorized to negate an action of the President." *Goldwater v. Carter*, 62 *L Ed 2d* 428 (1979), at 428.

41. "The Suggestion that this case presents a 'political question' is incompatible with this Court's unwillingness on previous occasions to decide whether one branch of government has impinged upon the power of another. If Congress, by appropriate formal action, had challenged the President's formal authority, . . . the resulting uncertainty would have serious consequences for our country. In that situation, it would be the duty of this Court to resolve the issue." Id. at 430.

42. Id. at 432.

43. See, for example, Bernard Schwartz, *Super Chief: Earl Warren and His Supreme Court* (New York: New York University Press, 1980); Howard Ball and Phillip Cooper, *Of Power and Rights: Justices Black and Douglas* (New York: Oxford University Press, 1991).

44. Mark V. Tushnet, "Darkness On the Edge of Town," *Yale Law Journal* 89, no.6, (May 1980): 1037.

45. Abram Chayes, "Public Law Litigation and the Burger Court," *Harvard Law Review* 96, no.4 (1986): 6.

46. William Lasser, *The Limits of Judicial Power* (Chapel Hill: University of North Carolina Press, 1988), p. 161.

47. See, for example, Phillip Cooper, *Hard Judicial Choices* (New York: Oxford University Press, 1988), for an excellent analysis of recent federal district court remedial decree activity.

48. There has been an ongoing discussion about the character and the limits of judicial review that has revolved around the use of terms such as interpretivist and noninterpretivist judicial review. Noninterpretivists are not bound by the language or the intent of the words of the Constitution and its Amendments. See, generally, John Hart Ely, *Democracy and Distrust: A Theory of Judicial Review* (Cambridge: Harvard University Press, 1980).

49. Paul Brest, "The Fundamental Rights Controversy: The Essential Contradictions of Normative Constitutional Scholarship," *Yale Law Journal* 90 (1981): 1064. For Brest, the countervailing view, held by conservatives, was that judicial review could only be used "to enforce explicit constitutional provisions or to ensure the integrity of representative government."

50. Edwin Meese, like his conservative counterparts on the Court and in the legal community, persons such as William Rehnquist and Robert Bork, for example, argued for a jurisprudence based on the original intent of the framers. He said that "the Constitution is the fundamental will of the people; that is why it is the fundamental law. To allow the courts to govern simply by what it views at the time as fair and decent, is a scheme of government no longer popular; the idea of democracy has suffered." Brennan, on the other hand, argued that the Meese position was "in truth . . . little more than arrogance cloaked in humility. It is arrogant to pretend that from our vantage we can gauge accurately the intent of the Framers on application of principle to specific, contemporary questions. . . . Those who would restrict claims of right to the values of 1789 . . . turn a blind eye to social progress." See Howard Ball, "The Convergence of Constitutional Law and Politics in the Reagan Administration: The Exhumation of the 'Jurisprudence of Original Intent' Doctrine," *Cumberland Law Review* 16 (Fall 1987).

51. David O'Brien interview with Potter Stewart, February 28, 1985, Washington, D.C.

52. David M. O'Brien, *Storm Center: The Supreme Court in American Politics* (New York: W. W. Norton, 1986), p. 215.

53. *Brown v. Allen*, 344 *U.S.* 443 (1953), at 540.

2

The Watergate Scandal Unfolds

Understanding the role of the Supreme Court in American politics and life calls for an understanding of the factual and social environmental underpinnings of litigation that comes to the high court for review by the justices. Although the Watergate Tapes litigation came to the Court in late May 1974, the justices, like all Americans, were fascinated and saddened by the tenor of the events that shook society prior to the formal legal arguments before the Court. As one scholar observed at the time, there was "no real possibility that the Court was unaware of these [Watergate-related] realities."[1] They, too, watched with deep concern as the tragedy unfolded before the national and international communities, in the courtrooms, in the senate committee rooms, at press conferences, in their daily newspapers, and live on national television and radio.

THE ABORTIVE BREAK-IN AT THE WATERGATE, APRIL 1972

Five persons broke into the Democratic party's national headquarters, located in the Watergate complex in Washington, D.C., on the evening of June 17, 1972.[2] They were there to plant electronic bugging devices in the telephones of top Democratic party officials. Once caught, these seven "plumbers," as they were called by the media—including one E. Howard Hunt, a former U.S. Central Intelligence Agency (CIA) agent and writer of spy novels who was working for the Nixon Re-Election Committee—were, in time, traced to the White House. That bungled effort to break into the Democratic party headquarters led to the demise of President Richard M. Nixon.

The five conspirators arrested that night were Bernard L. Barker, a Florida realtor and former CIA agent involved with the Bay of Pigs operation; Virgilio Gonzalez, a Miami locksmith who had come from Cuba prior to Fidel Castro's rise to power; Eugenio R. Martinez, who worked in Barker's real estate company and was an anti-Castro Cuban with CIA connections; James W. McCord, Jr., a security person with the Republican National Committee and the Committee to Re-Elect the President (chaired by former Nixon Attorney General John N. Mitchell); and Frank Sturgis, who had also worked at the CIA.

Hunt and another more eerie member of the group, G. Gordon Liddy (who was then counsel to the Finance Committee to Re-Elect the President and who had been a former FBI agent and former member of the White House staff), were arrested later and charged with the break-in along with five compatriots. "The job at Watergate had been a Hunt-Liddy job,"[3] and that meant White House involvement. Within hours of the arrest of the five burglars, high officials in the Nixon administration, including Chief Counselor for Domestic Affairs in the White House John Ehrlichman, and Nixon's Chief of Staff, H. R. Haldeman, were meeting to develop damage control plans.

In less than one week, on June 23, 1972 (as the nation was to find out the following summer when the tapes were released), President Nixon himself was to become irrevocably involved in the cover-up. The later revelation of White House involvement led to his decision to resign. On that fateful day, Nixon met with Bob Haldeman, who informed the president that Nixon's counsel John W. Dean III and former Attorney General and head of the Committee to Re-Elect the President John Mitchell had recommended that the CIA be called in to obstruct the FBI investigation of the Watergate break-in.

The CIA had to have instructions from Nixon to interfere in the name of national security, and Haldeman was there to seek Nixon's position. "All right, fine," responded Nixon to the Dean-Mitchell cover-up plan, saying, "Well, we protected [CIA Director Richard] Helms from one hell of a lot of things. Play it tough. That's the way they [Democrats] play it and that's the way we are going to play it."[4] From that moment on, regardless of whether Nixon consciously or unconsciously tore that conversation from his memory or whether the reality of his involvement remained in his mind, the president publicly pronounced himself innocent of any wrongdoing in the Watergate mess and privately told close friends and advisors, including his legal counsel, that he had not been involved in the Watergate affair.[5] Regardless of the psychological or pathological rationale, President Richard M. Nixon lied to the American people.

By late August 1972, with allegations about White House involvement in the break-in running on the media, Nixon announced that no one in his administration had been involved with the break-in. His investigation was conducted by his counsel, Dean. There was, as well, a Justice Department investigation of the break-in, the president remarked.

Shortly thereafter, Mitchell resigned as the Chairman of the Committee for the Re-Election of the President. As the tapes were to show much later, by the time of the trial of the plumbers, the White House began the futile efforts to cover-up its involvement in the break-in. Although President Nixon won reelection handily against his Democratic opponent, Senator George McGovern (D-SD), reporters and others did not let the Watergate matter end.

In the fall of 1972, the *Washington Post* reporting team of Robert Woodward and Carl Bernstein began their Watergate-related investigative reporting with stories of widespread Republican party "dirty tricks" against the Democratic candidates.[6] Their stories soon began to involve members of Nixon's inner circle, particularly Donald Segretti, who was hired by Nixon's own appointments secretary, Dwight Chapin, and Gordon Strachan, a White House staff aide who was paid by Herbert W. Kalbach, Nixon's personal attorney.

In a federal district court in January 1973, Hunt, Barker, Sturgis, Gonzalez and Martinez pleaded guilty.[7] In a criminal trial presided over by Chief Judge John J. Sirica, U.S. District Court, District of Columbia, Liddy and McCord were found guilty of the crimes of conspiracy and burglary and wiretapping violations.[8] Sentencing occurred in March 1973; Liddy received a prison sentence of more than six years.[9] Before McCord was sentenced, however, he wrote a letter to Sirica indicating that others were involved in the burglary and the conspiracy and that perjury had been committed.[10]

Sirica postponed sentencing until McCord had a chance to testify before a federal Grand Jury and before a special Senate committee, chaired by Senator Sam Ervin (D-NC), that was soon to begin investigating Watergate. In April 1973 Sirica granted McCord immunity from any further criminal prosecution, and the burglary participant began testifying before the Grand Jury.

THE WATERGATE BREAK-IN LEADS TO AN EFFORT TO COVER WHITE HOUSE INVOLVEMENT

Evidently, according to leaked information published in the *Washington Post* in early April 1973, McCord told the Select Committee that Mitchell personally approved the wiretap operation and that Dean had prior knowledge of the burglary and wiretap plans. The *New York Times* ran a story, which McCord told to the Grand Jury, that an attorney for the Nixon Re-Election Committee, Kenneth W. Parkinson, had given the burglars money after their arrest.[11]

The Ervin Committee, formally called the Senate Select Committee on Presidential Campaign Activities, began hearing testimony in public, on television, in May 1973. President Nixon at a televised press conference told the nation that all members of his White House staff would appear voluntarily to answer questions before the Ervin Committee.

More and more leaks began appearing in the press about White House staff involvement in the break-in. Mitchell and Dean were prominently mentioned in these stories, as was Ehrlichman. In late April, half a dozen White House staffers and others, including Nixon's re-election campaign manager,

Jeb Stewart Magruder, and Acting Director of the FBI, L. Patrick Grey (who was replaced by William D. Ruckelshaus) offered their resignations.[12]

On April 30, 1973, President Nixon made an effort to end the discussion by dismissing his chief advisors and others on his staff, including Attorney General Richard G. Kleindienst. Although Haldeman, Ehrlichman, Dean and others were fired and replaced by noncontroversial, competent persons (Elliot L. Richardson became the attorney general, Alexander Haig became the chief of staff, and Leonard Garment became Nixon's counsel), Watergate continued to invade homes across America and the world through the televised Ervin Committee sessions.[13]

UNCOVERING THE REALITY OF THE WATERGATE BREAK-IN: THE ERVIN SENATE COMMITTEE AND THE APPOINTMENT OF A SPECIAL PROSECUTOR

On May 12, 1972, nearly eleven months after the break-in occurred, the Senate, given the stories of executive personnel involvement in the Watergate scandal, approved by voice vote a resolution (introduced by Senator Charles Percy [R-IL]) calling for the president to appoint a special prosecutor, subject to confirmation by the Senate, to head the governmental investigation of Watergate. In an effort to minimize the damage being caused by Watergate, Nixon, on May 16, 1973, asked the Congress to create an independent commission to reform the electoral process. His attorney general, Elliot Richardson, in response to the Senate resolution calling for the action, announced on May 18, 1973 that he would appoint a long time colleague of his, Harvard Law Professor Archibald Cox, as special prosecutor for the Watergate investigation.[14] Cox, who had served as Solicitor General under Presidents John F. Kennedy and Lyndon B. Johnson, agreed to head the government's examination.

When Nixon appointed Richardson in April, he had given the attorney general the power and authority to name a special prosecutor "for matters arising out of [Watergate]." Under guidelines drawn by Richardson and Cox and printed in the *Federal Register* on May 25, 1973, the special prosecutor had virtual independence from the administration. He was given

> full authority for investigating and prosecuting offenses against the United States arising out of the unauthorized entry into Democratic National Committee headquarters at the Watergate, all offenses arising out of the 1972 presidential election for which the special prosecutor deems it necessary and appropriate to assume responsibility, allegations involving the President, members of the White House staff, or presidential appointees, and any other matters which he consents to have assigned to him by the attorney general.[15]

Cox's powers were considerable, including the decision whether to prosecute and the power to "determine whether or not to contest the assertion of 'executive privilege' or any other testimonial privilege." While he was technically in the Justice Department, Cox was to have "the greatest degree of independence that is consistent with the attorney general's statutory accountability for all matters falling within the jurisdiction of the Department of Justice." In addition to receiving promises of staff support to carry out his difficult mission, "the special prosecutor will not be removed from his duties except for extraordinary improprieties on his part."

Testifying before the Senate Judiciary Committee on May 23, 1973, Cox indicated that the only authority Richardson "retained is the authority to give me hell if I don't do the job." He viewed the guidelines as giving him "the best of both worlds," that is, independence from but strong support by the Justice Department and the attorney general. (Cox's tenure was to prove extremely difficult, in part because he was a Kennedy-Harvard-Democratic liberal trying to investigate the activities of persons, including Nixon, who had no love for "those kinds" of persons, and his investigation was terminated in the infamous Saturday night "massacre" in October 1973.[16])

On May 22, 1973, Nixon publicly admitted there was a White House cover-up of the Watergate affair. While claiming personal noninvolvement ("I had no prior knowledge of the Watergate bugging operation, or of any illegal surveillance activities for political purposes"), Nixon stated, "it now seems that . . . there were apparently wide-ranging efforts to limit the [Watergate] investigation [by Dean, Haldeman, Ehrlichman, and their associates] or to conceal the possible involvement of members of the Administration and the campaign committee."

The Ervin Committee hearings began at this time. Scores of witnesses appeared, from McCord to Mitchell and including Haldeman, Ehrlichman, Dean, Magruder and others from the Nixon White House and the re-election committee. Many gave conflicting testimony regarding the Watergate burglary and subsequent cover-up efforts. Cox urged the Committee to cease its activities or at least to postpone them for a few months lest probable criminal prosecutions be adversely affected by these televised sessions.[17] The Committee continued throughout the spring and into the summer of 1973, recessing August 7, 1973, after hearing testimony from thirty-three witnesses.

John Dean, the thirty-four year old attorney who had served as Nixon's White House counsel, was a star witness before the Senate committee for an entire week in June. He spoke of how he had warned the president of the cover-up cancer growing in the White House and directly accused the president of having known about the Watergate cover-up efforts since September 1972. Dean also linked the president with the actual break-in when he stated that he believed that Haldeman, who was aware of the surveillance efforts, probably reported them to Nixon.

THE EXISTENCE OF THE WATERGATE TAPES REVEALED: THE DRAMA HEIGHTENS IN CONGRESS AND THE FEDERAL COURTS

One event turned the Watergate scandal into the legal and political drama that ended with the resignation of Nixon in August 1974: The unexpected testimony from an administrator in the Federal Aviation Administration who had been a White House aide during the time of the break-in. The surprise witness testified on July 16, 1973 for only thirty minutes, yet the comments of Alexander Butterfield, a former CIA agent who had worked for Haldeman in the White House, caused a firestorm across the world that day. Simply, he revealed that President Nixon had taped all conversations in the Oval Room and in the Executive Office Building and that Butterfield's telephones had been tapped by Nixon since the spring of 1971. The White House confirmed his statements that the tapings had taken place and that the tapes were now in the possession of the president himself.

With that revelation both the Ervin Committee and Cox immediately sought the tapes.[18] On July 17, one day after the Butterfield public testimony, Ervin was writing the president requesting that "you provide the Committee with all relevant documents and tapes under control of the White House that relate to matters the Select Committee is authorized to investigate." Claiming executive privilege, however, Nixon refused to turn them over, instructing the Secret Service to withhold from the Senate all such documents and tapes. There is an inherent "executive privilege," he maintained, in the Constitutional separation of powers that allows the president to withhold such confidential information from the coordinate branches of government.

On July 23 Ervin told the Committee and the public watching and listening that Nixon

> owes an obligation to furnish a high standard of moral leadership to this nation and his constitutional duties, in my opinion, and undoubtedly his duty of affording moral leadership of the country places upon him some obligation under these circumstances. . . . I think that high moral leadership demands that the President make available to this country any information in the form of tapes or records which will shed some light [on the Watergate events].

Nixon did not bow to the senator from North Carolina. Furthermore, speaking through his deputy White House press secretary, Gerald Warren, the president cryptically indicated that he would consider accepting only a "definitive" ruling by the federal courts, and especially the U.S. Supreme Court, on the question of presidential privilege.[19] (He never did actually define what was meant by "definitive.")

Two subpoenas issued by the Committee were not honored

by Nixon, who wrote, "I cannot and will not consent to giving any investigatory body private presidential papers." The president then faced a federal court order signed by Judge Sirica that directed Nixon's lawyers to "show cause" why he would not comply with a subpoena seeking tapes and documents issued by Cox and the special prosecutor's office.[20]

Undaunted, Special Prosecutor Cox—working with a federal Grand Jury charged with determining whether additional criminal activities were associated with the Watergate break-in—had gone into federal court seeking permission to review, under Rule 17c of the Federal Rules of Criminal Procedure, nine of the tapes through the subpoena power of the federal courts. Nixon's response to the Cox subpoena was that, following a long line of presidential precedent, he was not turning the materials over to the office because of the "position that the president is not subject to compulsory process from the courts."

On August 13, 1978, Cox filed a memorandum in the U.S. District Court in the District of Columbia asking the court to compel Nixon to turn over the tapes to the special prosecutor's office. For Cox, writing in the brief,

> the President has an enforceable legal duty not to withhold material evidence from a grand jury. The grand jury occupies a fundamental position in the administration of public justice. There is no exception for the President from the guiding principle that the public, in the pursuit of justice, has a right to every man's evidence.[21]

On August 22, 1973, Harvard Law Professor Cox and Nixon's counsel, University of Texas Law Professor Charles Alan Wright, argued their respective points in Sirica's courtroom in the federal courthouse in the District of Columbia. For the president's counsel, courts were without power and authority to serve a sitting president with a subpoena. Further, if, on balance, a president decides that other interests, such as the concept of confidentiality, outweigh the presentment of evidence in a criminal proceeding, then that is the president's choice to make—without any judicial oversight. For Wright, the president was the "sole judge of executive privilege." The only remedy for presidential abuse of this trust in his judgment, noted the counsel, is impeachment.

Cox argued that the broad claim of executive privilege did not extend to the withholding of relevant evidence from a criminal justice action in a federal court. Quoting Justice Robert Jackson, Cox stated that "with all its defects . . . men have discovered no technique for long preserving free government except that the executive be under the law."

On August 29, 1973 Judge Sirica ordered Nixon to turn over the tapes to the federal judge for *in camera* inspection.[22] Sirica concluded that the Court had jurisdiction and that the matter was justiciable—that is, capable of resolution by the judiciary. While executive privilege was an ancient concept, it was not absolute and could be negated by the legitimate claim of a Grand Jury to all papers and other testimony that shed light on the Grand Jury's investigation into alleged criminal activities. "There can be executive privileges that will bar the production of evidence," Sirica wrote, and "the court is willing here to recognize and give effect to an evidentiary privilege based on the need to protest presidential privacy." But the Court had to examine the tapes to make the determination; "executive fiat is not the mode" for making such a determination. Sirica concluded:

> To paraphrase Chief Justice Marshall, if it be apparent that the tapes are irrelevant to the investigation, or that for state reasons they cannot be introduced into the case, the subpoena *duces tecum* would be useless. But if this be not apparent, if they *may* be important to the investigation, *may* be safely heard by the grand jury, if only in part, would it not be a blot on the page which records the judicial proceedings of this country, if, in a case of such serious import as this, the Court did not at least call for an inspection of evidence in chambers?

The president immediately chose not to comply with the Sirica order. Instead, he appealed. Cox and Wright took their legal show to the U.S. Court of Appeals, District of Columbia, on September 11, 1973. (Negotiations between Cox and Nixon's counsel, held shortly after these legal arguments were made in the appeals court, proved to be fruitless.)

The U.S. Court of Appeals in the District of Columbia heard the case *en banc* and, on October 12, 1973, upheld the Sirica judgment. By a 5:2 vote, the appeals court accepted Cox's contention that the tapes held "evidence critical to the grand jury's decisions as to whether and whom to indict." The majority also acknowledged that courts could indeed examine the validity of claims to executive privilege made by the president.

If the claim of absolute privilege was recognized, its mere invocation by the President or his surrogates could deny access to all documents in all the executive departments to all citizens and their representatives, including Congress, the courts as well as grand juries, state governments, state officials and all state subdivisions. The Freedom of Information Act could become nothing more than a legislative statement of unenforceable rights. Support for this kind of mischief simply cannot be spun from incantation of the doctrine of separation of powers.

Two of the federal appeals judges, Nixon appointees George E. MacKinnon and Malcolm Wilkey, filed dissenting opinions in the case. MacKinnon's partial dissent focussed on the "greatest vice of the decision. . . . [It] establish[es] a precedent that would subject every Presidential conference to the hazard of eventually being publicly exposed at the behest of some trial judge trying a civil or a criminal case." For Wilkey, the Court's intervention would destroy the "healthy equilibrium of tension" within government and, as such, was "oppressive." The Separation of Powers concept in the Constitution, he argued, created "protection against oppression," not "efficiency." His understanding of that concept allows the President to make such unilateral judgments "and it is the American people [not the federal courts] who will be the judge as to whether the President has made the right decision."

THE "SATURDAY NIGHT MASSACRE" AND THE "FIRESTORM" THAT ENSUED: OCTOBER 20–24, 1973

On national television on October 19, 1973, Nixon then offered the special prosecutor a compromise: providing Sirica and the Senate committee with summaries of the tapes (prepared by the White House) that would be verified by a senior friend of the president, Senator John C. Stennis (D-MS). Cox rejected the proposal, arguing that such an arrangement would "defeat the fair administration of justice." Furthermore, Cox indicated, at a dramatic October 20, 1972, press conference, that he had no intention of resigning from the office of special prosecutor. Richardson, the attorney general, agreed with Cox and disagreed with his boss, the president of the United States. He simply could not fire Cox because the special prosecutor had not committed any extraordinary improprieties.[23]

This refusal led to the infamous "Saturday Night Massacre" of October 20, in which Archibald Cox was fired as special prosecutor by Acting Attorney General Robert Bork, and the special prosecutor's office was (temporarily) abolished.[24] (Elliot Richardson and William Ruckelshaus had both resigned rather than fire the Watergate special prosecutor; Solicitor General Bork implemented the presidential order.) Upon being relieved by Bork, Cox said that "whether we shall continue to be a government of laws and not of men is now for Congress and ultimately the American people to decide."

A "firestorm"[25] of protest broke out across the nation as a consequence of these stunning events and, within four days the president's attorney informed Judge Sirica that the president would turn the tapes over to him. Said Charles Alan Wright, a University of Texas law professor who was acting as one of the president's counsel, before Judge Sirica on October 23, 1973:

> I am authorized to say that the President of the United States would comply in all respects with the order of August 29 as modified by the order of the court of appeals. . . . This President does not defy the law, and he has authorized me to say he will comply in full with the orders of the court.

The "massacre" and the subsequent outcry against Nixon led to the initiation of impeachment conversations in Congress for the first time in a century, conversations which has been muted or halted months earlier because Congress had not been jolted into the realization that Nixon might have committed impeachable offenses.[26] By October 26th, given the firestorm of protest, Nixon announced that Bork would soon appoint a new special prosecutor. On November 2, 1973, Bork reestablished the Watergate Special Prosecution Force and appointed Leon Jaworski as special prosecutor. In an Order published in the Federal Register, Bork gave Jaworski "full authority [to] contest the assertion of 'executive privilege' or any other testimonial privilege." Pointedly, Bork noted that Nixon could not fire Jaworski, except for extraordinary improprieties, and only after consulting with and getting the approval of six of the eight top leaders in the Congress.[27]

Given the massacre and new discoveries and disclosures, such as two missing tapes and one that had been erased by an unknown person or persons, in February 1974 the House of Representatives asked the Judiciary Committee to begin impeachment hearings. In March, after reviewing portions of the six tapes finally released by the president, the federal Grand Jury (led by the new Watergate special prosecutor, Leon Jaworski), handed down indictments against seven persons[28] and secretly named Richard M. Nixon as an unindicted co-conspirator. The federal Grand Jury asked that information against Nixon be turned over to the House Judiciary Committee that was examining the impeachment question.

MOVING TOWARD THE SUPREME COURT AND THE POSSIBILITY OF A DEFINITIVE RULING BY THE HIGH COURT

Both the Judiciary Committee of the House, chaired by Congressman Peter Rodino (D-NJ) and the special prosecutor's office requested additional tapes from Nixon's lawyers. In April 1974 Jaworski went into federal district court and asked Chief Judge Sirica to order Nixon to turn over an additional sixty-four tapes. Nixon, once more claiming executive privilege, refused to hand over the tapes to either Rodino or Jaworski. The president's lawyers, again in Sirica's court, reargued the executive privilege position and also claimed that the matter was an intra-branch dispute between Nixon and a subordinate (Jaworski).

In late May Sirica ordered the president to turn the tapes over to him for an *in camera* inspection. Nixon appealed. On May 24, 1974 Jaworski took the dramatic step of bypassing the Court of Appeals and asking the Supreme Court to grant certiorari under expedited review as permitted in Rule 20 of the Supreme Court's Rules.

The Court could have declined the invitation extended to it by the special prosecutor. As a matter of discretion, if not of jurisdiction (which could have involved the separation of powers and the "political question" doctrines), the justices could have rejected the petition and allowed the Court of Appeals to hear the arguments. Given the issue's "delicacy" as well as the "pendency of impeachment proceedings," there could have emerged from the Court a "counsel of restraint, deliberate speed rather than majestic instancy."[29] Only five times in the nation's history had the Court granted expedited review under a Rule 20 protocol.

But the Court took *Nixon*, as will be seen, "because the case needed to be cracked—and soon—and it was not clear that it otherwise would be; and because the Court felt a responsibility to the nation to bring this about."[30] Justice Brennan, who led the successful effort in the Court to hear the case in an expedient fashion, clearly underlined the validity of this early observation when he wrote, in 1988, "[We] felt strongly that the nation would think we had 'let the people down' if we didn't bypass. . . . [We had to act] lest the nation lose all confidence in the criminal justice system."[31]

And so it was that, about two years after the initial abortive effort by some plumbers to bug the Democratic National party headquarters in the Watergate complex, the members of the U.S. Supreme Court became involved in the case of *United States v. Nixon*.

NOTES

1. Paul J. Mishkin, "Great Cases and Soft Law: A Comment on *United States v. Nixon*," *UCLA Law Review* 22, no.6 (1974), at 78.

2. Unless otherwise noted, the chronological data and public statements used in the chapter are from Congressional Quarterly, *Watergate: Chronology of a Crisis* (Washington, D.C.: Congressional Quarterly Press, 1975).

3. Theodore White, *Breach of Faith: The Fall of Richard Nixon* (New York: Atheneum, 1975), p. 161.

4. Ibid., p. 164. White noted, at this point: "And, with that quick exchange the President was impeachable." In 1990, a reflective Nixon commented about that June 23, 1973 conversation. "In my talk with Haldeman, I made the inexcusable error of following the recommendation from some members of my staff—some of whom, I later learned, had a personal stake in covering up the facts." Nixon interview, *Time*, April 2, 1990, p. 37.

5. See, generally, Bob Woodward and Carl Bernstein, *The Final Days* (New York: Simon and Schuster, 1976).

6. See, generally, Bob Woodward and Carl Bernstein, *All The President's Men* (New York: Simon and Schuster, 1974), for an excellent analysis of the events associated with the Watergate break-in and cover-up.

7. Walter Rugabar, "Watergate Trial Hears Hunt Offer to Plead Guilty," *New York Times*, January 11, 1973; Walter Rugabar, "More Guilty Pleas Hinted Amid Watergate Secrecy," *New York Times*, January 13, 1973; Walter Rugabar, "Four More Admit Guilt As Spies in Watergate," *New York Times*, January 16, 1973; Lawrence Meyer, "E. Howard Hunt Pleads Guilty in Watergate Case," *Washington Post*, January 11, 1973; C. Bernstein and B. Woodward, "Plea Shifts Hinted in Watergate Case," *Washington Post*, January 16, 1973.

8. Walter Rugabar, "Liddy and McCord Are Guilty of Spying on the Democrats," *New York Times*, January 31, 1973.

9. Walter Rugabar, "Liddy Sentenced for Defying Jury: Up to 18 Months Are Added to Watergate Jail Term," *New York Times*, April 4, 1973.

10. Walter Rugabar, "Watergate Spy Says Defendants Were Under 'Political Pressure' To admit Guilt and Keep Silent: To Talk To Judge," *New York Times*, March 24, 1973.

11. Seymour Hersh, "McCord Reported Linking Payoffs to GOP Lawyer and Says He Believes Parkinson Paid Bugging Defendants," *New York Times*, April 9, 1973.

12. Walter Rugabar, "Grey Quits the FBI, Ruckelshaus Named; A Justice Department Memo Says Liddy and Hunt Raided Office of Ellsberg's Psychiatrist," *New York Times*, April 28, 1973. George Lardner Jr. and Carroll Kilpatrick, "Magruder Resigns U.S. Job," *Washington Post*, April 27, 1973.

13. Other White House staff personnel who resigned during the last week in April and the first weeks in May 1973 included Egil Krogh Jr., a former member of the Committee to Re-Elect the President, Gordon C. Strachan, Haldeman's link to the re-election committee, Robert Odle Jr., Dwight Chapin, Kenneth Rietz, and David R. Young.

14. Richardson was a former student of Cox and called his professor on May 17, 1973, to ask if he would take over the difficult job of special prosecutor. Cox was sixty-one years old at that time.

15. Department of Justice Order No. 517-73, 38 *Federal Register* 14,688, Adding 28 CFR Section 0.37, Appendix to Subpart G-1.

16. During the October "massacre," Cox was fired by Acting Attorney General Robert Bork after Richardson and Ruckelshaus resigned rather than fire Cox.

17. Cox went into federal court for a ruling that the Senate hearings be delayed or be held in secret because persons indicted by the Grand Jury would not be able to have a fair trial due to their public appearances before the Senate committee. After Judge Sirica ruled against Cox's motions, there were no appeals. On June 12 Cox said: "I regret the outcome, but to press the legal argument further would risk unduly delaying proceedings and divert attention from our essential tasks."

18. By this time Cox's staff had identified five Watergate-related areas of illegal activity that they would bring to the Grand Jury: (1) the break-in and cover-up itself, (2) the burglarizing activities of other "plumbers," (3) the ITT pay-off scandal, (4) illegal campaign contributions, and (5) various dirty tricks carried out against unsuspecting Democratic candidates by the Committee to Re-Elect the President staff. See Howard Ball, *No Pledge of Privacy: The Watergate Tapes Litigation* (New York: Kennikat Press, 1977), p. 21.

19. Mishkin, "Great Cases and Soft Law," p. 87.

20. Cox could not accept Nixon's use of, as Cox described it, a "blanket claim of privilege to withhold this evidence from a grand jury." For the harried special prosecutor's office, Nixon's position was "without legal foundation."

21. Cox cited at this point *United States v. Burr*, 25 *Fed Cases* 187 (1807).

22. See Ball, *No Pledge of Privacy*, for a detailed examination of the litigation surrounding the Cox request for the tapes.

23. At one point during the week prior to the dismissal of Cox, Richardson attended a White House strategy session on the issue chaired by Alexander Haig. Noting the intense ardor of Haig and others, he wrote: "I wondered whether I was the only sane man in the

room or whether I was the only one who was crazy." Quoted in Ball, *No Pledge of Privacy*, p. 37.

24. Leon Jaworski, a well-known trial lawyer and former president of the American Bar Association from Texas, was named the new special prosecutor on November 1, 1973, replacing Cox. He was promised full cooperation in his efforts, including the use of presidential documents, by the new attorney general, William B. Saxbe. Furthermore, due to the Cox firing, Jaworski was assured that he would not be fired unless a substantial majority of an eight-person ad hoc joint congressional judiciary committee agreed with the administration that he should be discharged.

25. The phrase was coined by Nixon's chief of state, General Alexander P. Haig, quoted in *Time*, November 15, 1973, p. 13.

26. In *Nader v. Bork*, 366 *F Supp* 104 (1974), District Court Judge Gerhard Gessell, U.S. District Court, District of Columbia, ruled that Cox's firing was illegal because Bork had simply relied on verbal instructions from Haig and the president and had not found nor presented any "extraordinary improprieties" committed by Cox that warranted summary dismissal.

27. Department of Justice Order No. 551-73, 38 *Federal Register* 30, 738 (November 2, 1973); Department of Justice Order 554-73 38 *Federal Register* (November 19, 1973).

28. The seven were John Mitchell, H. R. Haldeman, John Ehrlichman, Charles Colson, Robert Mardian, Gordon Strachan, and Kenneth Parkinson.

29. Freund, "Forward: On Presidential Privilege," *Harvard Law Review* 88 (November 1974): 14.

30. Mishkin, "Great Cases and Soft Law," p. 76.

31. Letter, William J. Brennan, Jr. to Howard Ball, January 4, 1988.

3

The Supreme Court in 1974: Personae, Process, and Politics

Richard M. Nixon ran for the presidency in 1968 with what one scholar labeled the "hot campaign issue: the Supreme Court."[1] He ran against not only the Democratic candidate, Hubert Humphrey, but also against chief justice of the United States Earl Warren and the super chief's liberal allies on the high bench. Said Nixon, in July, 1968, on the campaign trail: "I believe in a strict interpretation of the Supreme Court's functions. In essence this means I believe we need a Court which looks upon its functions as being that of interpretation rather than of breaking through into new areas that are really the prerogative of the Congress of the United States."[2]

In part, Nixon's campaign strategy was to run against an attitude of the Court that had existed throughout the Warren years. That judicial feeling was "that somehow it is the Court's special obligation to save the nation from episodes of constitutional crisis."[3] (Ironically, that attitude pervaded the conference sessions held during the months of May through July 1974 and, even though it was known as Nixon's Court or the Burger

Court, the brethren's response to the crisis of Watergate proved to be the equal of similar responses of the Warren Court to crisis.)

Taking advantage of the public's fears about the spread of crime, Nixon's campaign rhetoric charged the Warren Court with being soft on criminals and promised that, if elected, he would see to it that the Court was turned around.

> Over and over again, Nixon said on the hustings, Let us always respect, as I do, our courts and those who serve on them. But let us also recognize that some of our courts in their decisions have gone too far in weakening the peace forces against the criminal forces in this country and we must act to restore that balance.[4]

It was "good politics"[5] to attack the Court in 1968 and Nixon attacked the Warren "bunch" with as much gusto as he could muster. As one scholar observed, Nixon "sensed the national mood and sensed that the public was willing to have the Supreme Court shoulder part of the blame. . . . Nixon was convinced that the Court was politically vulnerable and he would act shrewdly on that knowledge.[6]

It was clear that, if elected, Nixon would pack the Court in order to nullify the doctrines developed by the liberal Warren Court.[7] Once in office, Nixon indeed had four occasions to create the Court in his own ideological image. Shortly after he became president, Nixon was able to name a new chief justice, Warren Earl Burger, to replace Earl Warren. After that appointment, Nixon had to endure the defeat of the two nominees[8] he had put forward to replace the tragic Abe Fortas, a judge who was forced off the Court by the Nixon/U.S. Attorney General John Mitchell strategy.[9] Harry A. Blackmun was finally confirmed by the Senate in April 1970.

When Justices Hugo Black and John M. Harlan II resigned in September 1971 within days of each other due to failing health (both passed away within months of their resignation), Nixon was able to nominate and have the U.S. Senate confirm two justices: Lewis Powell, Jr. and someone from his own Justice Department, William Rehnquist. When the 1972 term of the Supreme Court commenced on the first Monday in October, people were referring to the U.S. Supreme Court as either the Nixon or the Burger Court.

The 1973 term of the Court was the second full term of the nine-person "[Nixon/]Burger Court."[10] The Court was fractionalized, partly because the four new justices had been on the bench for such a brief time. Of the 144 decisions announced during that term, a majority of them were split 5:4 or 6:3.

On constitutional decisions, the conservative Nixon quartet plus Justices Byron White (85 percent) and Potter Stewart (82 percent) voted as a block and frustrated the other group. The "liberals," consisting of Justices William O. Douglas, William J. Brennan, Jr., and Thurgood Marshall, voted as a bloc 74 percent of the time on constitutional issues—and lost on most of them.[11] It took a truly exceptional case to unite such a diverse and fragmented group.

THE PERSONAE

The members of the family sitting on the Court in May 1974 included a Roosevelt appointee (William O. Douglas), two Eisenhower appointees (William J. Brennan, Jr. and Potter Stewart), a Kennedy appointee (Byron R. White), a Johnson appointee (Thurgood Marshall), and the four Nixon appointees. It was a very diverse group of personalities; these were also jurists whose jurisprudence clashed across all issues, from judicial role to criminal justice issues.

Chief Justice Burger was an extremely strong supporter of executive power generally and of President Nixon in particular. In Burger's eyes, Watergate was purely a

> political battle, a way for certain political elements to do what they had failed to accomplish in the 1972 election. . . . Now, the news media were on a witch-hunt trying to tie the actions of his aides to the President himself. The newspapers had become character assassins, the Chief declared. All the innuendo, distortion, hearsay and sensational headlines were vindictive. . . . 'Apart from the morality,' the Chief concluded, 'I don't see what they did wrong.'[12]

Warren E. Burger, born in Minnesota, graduated from St. Paul College of Law and came to Washington, D.C., to work in the Justice Department and, in 1956, as an Eisenhower appointee, he was appointed to the Court of Appeals in the District of Columbia. A conservative on the Court of Appeals, especially in criminal justice matters, he became a favorite of the men in the Nixon White House, and, when Earl Warren finally retired, the president, without really ever having met Burger, immediately nominated the white-maned, distinguished looking conservative jurist to be chief justice of the United States.

William O. Douglas, the senior member of the Court, began his tenure in 1939. He and Hugo Black were at the very center of a three decade long revolution in American constitutional law that saw an expansion of both the powers of the governors to deal with economic and social problems as well as an expansion of the constitutional liberties and rights of individuals.[13] A pure iconoclast, a lover of the outdoors who grew to adulthood by overcoming poverty and serious illness, Douglas was a law professor at Yale and Columbia during the height of the Legal Realism movement. He was an appointed "New Dealer" who had served on the Securities and Exchange Commission, including a stint as chairman of the SEC.

A close friend of Franklin D. Roosevelt (and other presidents), he had been nominated by Roosevelt in 1939 to replace a hero of his, Louis D. Brandeis. Douglas had seen Richard Nixon as "the enemy" for more than thirty years, from his bitter congressional campaign against Helen Gahagen Douglas in 1946 to his "Red baiting" activities in Congress. Douglas recalled an incident that reflected the character of the relationship between the two protagonists:

> Douglas told friends how Nixon reminded him of a speech Douglas had given more than thirty years before to Nixon's law-school class at Duke University. Nixon said the speech had been so impressive that it inspired his own political career. Hearing that, Douglas said, was the most upsetting moment in his life, the only time he actually felt 'suicidal.'[14]

Reviewing the Douglas files, it was clear that the senior associate justice did not like President Richard M. Nixon. In May 1973, more than a year before the Watergate litigation came to the Court, Douglas was asking friends of his—such as, former owner of the *Denver Post* Palmer Hoyt; a sitting U.S. Court of Appeals judge for the Ninth Circuit, James M. Carter; and, through Judge Carter, prominent San Francisco attorney Roger Kent—for information about Nixon

> in order to get to the bottom of the story that some of RMN's aides [H. R. Haldeman, Maurice Stans, Murray Chotiner, and Roger Kalmbach among others] were prosecuted in a state court in California as a result of conduct in the 1962 campaign in which Pat Brown won? I have been hearing about it for days, but from no one who knows first hand.[15]

The contacts quickly responded to the Douglas inquiry by providing him with data showing that, to use Douglas's language, "Our Hero [Nixon] was not the victim of unsuspected associates. He knew his way around without help."[16] Given that President Nixon and his attorney general, Mitchell, were instrumental in encouraging impeachment proceedings in Congress against Douglas in 1970 through their man in the House of Representatives, Gerald Ford (R-MI), it is easy to see why Douglas did not hold great affection for the president.[17]

It is equally clear that, by the time of the 1974 *Nixon* litigation, Douglas and the new chief justice, Warren Earl Burger, were often at odds on substantive as well as procedural issues. After the super chief, Earl Warren, finally retired in 1969, Nixon tapped Burger, who was then sitting on the U.S. Court of Appeals in the District of Columbia, for the center seat. Burger was a conservative jurist who espoused "law and order" themes during his tenure in Washington, D.C., in the Eisenhower Justice Department and as a federal judge. Burger said he saw the president as an "extraordinarily bright man."[18] While "Burger was the casting director's ideal of a Chief Justice,"[19] he was not a very bright jurist nor was he the respected small group leader, even though, Douglas noted, "He loved the administrative aspects of the office. He loved being Chief."[20]

This love of administrative control led to a serious, lengthy clash between Douglas and Burger. The chief tried to upset the Court tradition of the chief's assigning opinions only if he had voted with the majority in the Conference. In the spring of 1972 Douglas began to chastise Burger for trying to assign an opinion to Justice White, although Burger had voted with the minority. "With all due respect, I think Powell [one of the five who had joined to agree on the outcome] represents the consensus. I have not canvassed everybody but I am sure that Byron . . . will not get a court."[21] Powell ultimately did write the opinion for the Court in a watershed Fourth Amendment case of *United States v. U.S. District Court*.[22]

In another missive on the same issue directed at the chief, Douglas tried, again, to educate Burger on the custom of opinion writing in the Court. Douglas had just found out that Burger, although in the minority again, had assigned himself the task of writing the majority opinion in the free-speech-in-shopping-centers case, *Lloyd Corporation v. Tanner*.[23] Douglas, as senior justice in the majority, had already assigned the writing task to Justice Thurgood Marshall. "Historically," Douglas wrote,

> the Chief Justice has made the assignment if he is in the majority. Historically, the senior in the majority assigns the opinion if the Chief Justice is in the minority.[24] You led the Conference battle against affirmance and that is your privilege. But it is also the privilege of the majority, absent the Chief Justice, to make the assignment. Hence *Lloyd* was assigned and is assigned. . . . If the Conference wants to authorize you to assign all opinions, that will be a new procedure. Though opposed to it, I will acquiesce. But unless we make a frank reversal in our policy, any group in the majority should and must make the assignment. . . . *Lloyd* stays assigned to Thurgood.[25]

The chief backed off, but did not respond to the Douglas practice of coldly "lashing out" at his peers.[26]

"Under Burger," Douglas reflected, "there was pressure to join ranks."[27] For Douglas, who was ever anxious to depart humid Washington, D.C., this was always a grating situation. He responded appropriately by finishing his Court work quickly—and then leaving D.C. for Goose Prairie, Washington, and other faraway places. Douglas continued that practice during the time the Court was hearing, debating, and drafting the *Nixon* opinion.

William J. Brennan, Jr. had been appointed to the Court by President Dwight Eisenhower in 1956. At the time, Brennan was a member of New Jersey's Supreme Court. Eisenhower was later to state that Brennan's and Warren's appointments to the Supreme Court had been the two greatest mistakes he had made in his political life. Although Brennan had been a student of Frankfurter's when they were both at Harvard Law School, Brennan almost immediately gravitated to the side of the person he would later refer to as "Super Chief," Earl Warren. After Warren's retirement in 1969, Brennan "tried above all to keep the Warren flame burning."[28] He was to become, after Douglas's departure from the Court in 1975, the most dynamic of the court liberals.

From the very beginning of the Watergate drama, Brennan, the consummate Court consensus builder (and recipient of all kinds of gossip about the other justices' views on pending matters), counted the votes for and against the president when the tapes case came to the Court. "The results of his unofficial poll indicated that the vote might have been anything but 'definitive.' "[29]

Potter Stewart, a moderate Republican from Ohio, was a young forty-three when he was appointed to the Supreme Court by President Eisenhower in 1958. He disdained the labels associated with his peers' actions. Stewart was, he maintained, neither a liberal nor a conservative: "I am a [pragmatic] lawyer. . . . And I find it impossible to know what they mean when they [the labels "liberal" and "conservative"] are carried over to judicial work."[30] By the time of *Nixon*, Stewart had shown himself to be a pragmatic centrist on the Court; he had grown increasingly "skeptical about a President run amok."[31]

Byron White, or "Whizzer" White, as professional football fans knew him in the late 1930s (who followed his all-star playing in the National Football League), was an attorney in Colorado who had managed the 1960 Kennedy presidential campaign. In 1961 he was brought into the Kennedy Justice Department and, one year later, was nominated by President Kennedy to serve on the Supreme Court. While a pragmatic jurist on many issues, by 1974 White had shown himself to be, in Blackmun's words, "distinctly a conservative" in criminal justice litigation.[32] Ironically, because of his attitudes about the nature of the criminal justice process, White was concerned about the president's rejection of the subpoena's request to turn over information for use in a criminal trial.

Thurgood Marshall, who first came to the Court as the director of the NAACP's Legal Defense and Educational Fund and as lead NAACP counsel in numerous race segregation cases in the 1940s and 1950s (primarily as chief counsel in the *Brown* arguments and briefs before the Court) had served the national government on the U.S. Court of Appeals and as solicitor general before being appointed on the Supreme Court by President Lyndon B. Johnson in 1967. The first black to serve in this position, he was a fiery liberal prior to his elevation to the Court and remained so after joining.

Harry Blackmun was the second Nixon appointment to the Supreme Court in 1970 after the full Senate embarrassingly defeated the president's "southern" candidates, Clement F. Haynesworth, Jr. (U.S. Court of Appeals–Fourth Circuit) and G. Harold Carswell (U.S. Court of Appeals–Fifth Circuit), because of their prior questionable ethical and discriminatory behavior. A friend of Burger's who, like the chief, grew up in Minnesota, Blackmun had been a Court of Appeals judge for more than a decade before being tapped by Nixon after the Haynesworth-Carswell debacle. Blackmun had developed a conservative voting record at the time of the 1974 litigation involving the president, had voted in a manner that mirrored the chief's patterns, and was often referred to, derisively, as the second half of the Minnesota Twins. By the time of *Roe v. Wade*[33] and *Sierra Club v. Morton*,[34] however, Blackmun had moved quite dramatically apart from his chief. The break actually began in 1974 during the *Nixon* litigation when, as will be shown in a subsequent chapter, Blackmun completely revised—to the chagrin of the Chief—Burger's statement of the facts in the tapes litigation.

In August 1973, almost a year before the litigation came to the Court, Blackmun had told an audience of lawyers and judges at the American Bar Association that Watergate had created an atmosphere in which the "very glue of our ship of state seems about to become unstuck." He feared that "grave damage" had been done to the democratic process because of the scandal. "The pall of Watergate," he noted, "is upon us."[35]

Lewis Powell was the Nixon appointee who, in Blackmun's language, "held the [Court's] center."[36] Nixon's lone Democratic selection had come to the Court at age sixty-four after a successful career in private practice in Richmond, Virginia and after holding the presidency of the conservative American Bar Association. According to sources in the Court during the fateful 1973 term, it was "difficult to tell where Powell stood" on the Nixon issue.[37]

William Rehnquist was the arch-conservative on the Supreme Court in 1974. A successful attorney in Phoenix, Arizona, Rehnquist was brought into the first Nixon administration's Justice Department as an assistant attorney general (head of the office of legal counsel). He, with Powell, was nominated by Nixon to replace two major figures in American jurisprudence, Hugo L. Black and John M. Harlan Jr. Because of his close association with some of the defendants in the *Nixon* litigation, he recused himself from participation in the case and did not really have any substantive involvement in the Court's deliberations.

There were, looking at the Court brethren in another way, three recognized "liberal" bloc justices (Douglas, Brennan, and Marshall), three "conservative" jurists (Rehnquist, Burger, and Blackmun), and three "moderate" or swing justices (Stewart, White, and Powell). In short, the ideological divisions on the court at the time of the Jaworski gambit strongly suggested that, at best, there would be a divided court ruling—if it took the case at all on an expedited basis—on the merits.

Certainly the president's lawyers expected such an outcome; they thought the Rule 20 certiorari petition would be denied.[38] Even Leon Jaworski, the Watergate special prosecutor, and Phillip Lacovara, the counsel to the special prosecutor, "thought that it would be a 5:3 with William O. Douglas writing the majority opinion."[39] (One commentator on Watergate did note, however, that "Fred Buzhardt and Al Haig knew that as soon as the court bypassed the [U.S. Court of] Appeals, they were fairly certain that the President would lose."[40])

THE PROCESS OF JUDGING IN THE SUPREME COURT

"The business of the court," said Potter Stewart, "is to give institutional opinions for its decisions."[41] The opinion of the Supreme Court is the vehicle through which the Court expresses its institutional decision. The Court has complete control over its docket and very carefully grants *certiorari* or notes jurisdiction in *appeals as of right*. In a typical Term of the Supreme Court, which begins the first Monday in October, the justices will receive more than 5,000 petitions for appellate review of decisions handed down in state supreme courts or in federal courts of appeals. In that same Term the Court will hear, on the merits, about 120 cases. The balance, almost 95 percent of the petitions received by the clerk of the Court, are either dismissed or denied by the Court.

During the Term, the justices gather in the large, ornate courtroom to hear oral arguments involving these cases being reviewed on the merits. The oral argument takes place in two week-cycles. When not sitting in public and hearing arguments, the members of the Court are working in chambers on cases and controversies that have been or will be argued before the justices that term. (See exhibit 3.1).

In the Supreme Court, the process of decision making, that is, arriving at consensus on particular opinions, can also be understood by viewing it as two distinct phases of court work: the group phase and the individual phases.

The *group phase* activities include the public oral argument and the Court's secret Conference Sessions. The Conference Session is the heart of the judicial decision-making process. "The most important work of the Supreme Court . . . occurs behind the scenes, particularly at the Conference Session, where the Justices discuss and vote on cases."[42] It is in these sessions, now held on Wednesday afternoons and all day on Fridays, that initial questions of jurisdiction and justiciability are raised and where, after oral argument is heard, the justices discuss their views on the litigation and take their initial soundings on the outcome of the case before them.

In the Conference Session, after the discussions end, the as-

Exhibit 3.1
Judicial Decisional Flowchart: U.S. Supreme Court

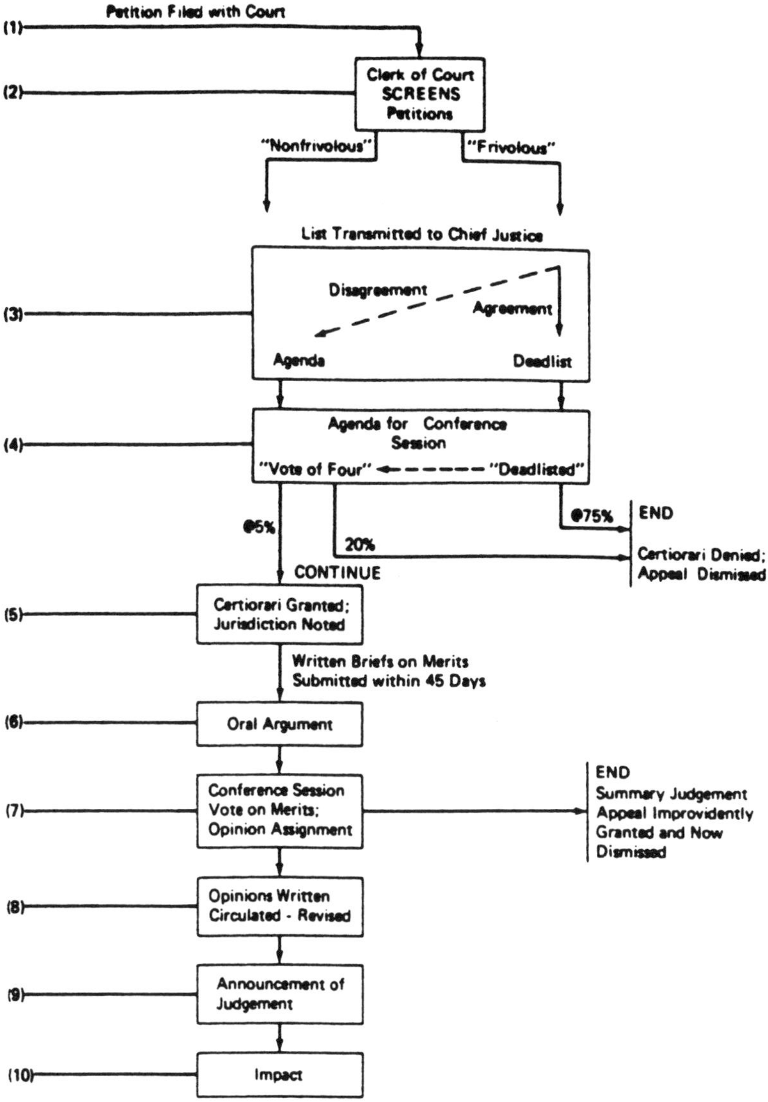

Source: Howard Ball, *Courts and Politics*, 2d. ed. (Englewood Cliffs, NJ: Prentice-Hall, 1987), p. 269

signments of opinions are made to specific justices based on the attitudes expressed by the group on a particular case. During the term of the Court, from October until early July, there are twenty to twenty-three Wednesday (afternoon) and Friday sessions, which coincide with the weeks the Court schedules oral argument.

Summoned to the Conference Session by a buzzer rung by the chief justice (as was the practice in Burger's Chief Justiceship), justices shake hands with their colleagues, then sit down to work on the crowded agenda they received earlier in the week. The formal order of business in the Conference Session runs as follows:

1. Appeals petitions,
2. Writs of certiorari,
3. *In forma pauperis* (prisoner) petitions, and disposition of cases heard in oral argument that week.

It takes a formal "vote of four" of the nine justices to have petitions and writs accepted by the Court for further consideration. As Justice Brennan once said, "Only an exceptional case raising a significant federal question commands the review" by the Court.[43] Justice Harlan said that, in this judgmental exercise, "frequently the question of whether a case is 'courtworthy' is more a matter of 'feel' than of precisely ascertainable standards."[44]

The agenda is drawn up by the chief justice and his administrative staff. Its implementation is a manifestation of the task and social leadership skills, or lack of skills, of the chief.[45] The chief justice has to direct the group to the central issues, make sure that they are discussed in a timely manner, and then bring the discussion to a close in order to get to the rest of the agenda.

The Wednesday session is generally a discussion of the cases heard in oral argument earlier that week. The Friday Conference Session disposes of the rest of the cases heard that week and initiates action on the petitions for Court review. No one but the justices are involved in the Conference Session; notes are taken by individual justices and maintained or not for posterity based on the individual's views about such politically and philosophically intimate record maintenance.[46]

In the Conference Session the "mettle of a justice is tested, for here he must meet his colleagues in the rough and tumble of free discussion."[47] In the *Nixon* case the Conference Sessions were critical in the initial judgment to grant expedited certiorari under Rule 20 and in the subsequent group discussions on the substantive issue of executive privilege. Although a number of justices opposed bringing the case to the Court under Rule 20, they participated fully and quite effectively once the case was in the Court. As Justice Black once noted, the jurisdictional vote "is not the equivalent of a final vote on the merits."[48]

The "vote" taken in conference is not the final, binding vote. Indeed, in reality no actual vote is taken. What does occur is the announcement, during the discussion of the case, of the justice's initial position on the merits of that litigation. After listening to the conversation and taking notes on the justices' views of the case being discussed, there is, in effect, a tallying up of positions.

Traditionally, when discussing a case heard earlier in the week, the chief justice begins the discussion with his or her views of the case and where he or she falls with regard to disposition. After the chief finishes, in order of seniority (the most senior speaking first) the associate justices make their observations and announce how they would dispose of the case. In a recent letter, Chief Justice Rehnquist wrote that "the discussion and voting at Conference are combined in one presentation by each Justice (unless the Justice chooses to 'pass'), and that these presentations proceed in order from the Chief Justice to the Junior Justice. . . . I talked this over with Justice Brennan, who has the longest service of any present member of the Court. He confirms that since he came to the Court in the fall of 1956, the procedure has been as I describe it to you."[49]

After all nine have spoken on the instant case, the Court moves on to the next. Because the justices all keep conference notes and all have docket books in which to record these judicial assessments, the opinion assignment generally occurs after the Conference Session ends.

If the chief justice's views are shared by another four, then the chief makes the decision about who will write the opinion. If the chief's views are shared by a minority of colleagues, then the senior associate justice whose views are similar to the majority determines the opinion-writing assignment. (As was noted earlier, this issue caused a deep rift between Burger and the senior associate justice, Douglas). It is critical to note that these initial observations are tentative, not binding. Given the fluidity of judicial choice in the Court,[50] there are occasional changes in position.

The fact that a justice, at a conference held the previous term, did not vote to hear a case that has come to the Court (because at least four of that justice's peers voted to grant certiorari) does not disqualify that justice from participating in the discussion on the merits. "I have frequently voted to reverse cases where I voted against bringing them before our Court for review," wrote Justice Black. "This is so because that for many reasons a vote to grant certiorari is not the equivalent of a final vote on the merits. And the same thing may frequently be true about dismissal of an appeal."[51]

There are a great many interactions between the justices after the Conference Sessions, and these lead to the occasional switch in a legal position. Persuaded by arguments in conference, or in the written opinions circulated after the Conference Session ends, a justice will move in one direction; after conversations with colleagues and after reading or writing one of the opinions that circulate for each case, he or she may begin to move in the opposite direction. Justice Brennan has said:

> I have had to convert more than one of my proposed majority opinions into a dissent before the final opinion was announced. I have also, however, had the satisfying experience of rewriting a dissent as a majority opinion of the court.[52]

Black summed up this phenomenon when he wrote: "My votes at conference are never final. They are tentative and I am always ready to change the vote if I reach the conclusion that my vote was wrong."[53]

The *individual phase* of the judicial decision-making process is the lonely time spent by each justice reviewing the briefs, oral arguments, and memos compiled by the clerks and staff in preparation for either writing an opinion or responding to one circulated by some of the other justices. The justice reads information about pending cases; there is also preparation for the next cycle of oral presentations in the Court. General homework, catch-up and writing is done in this phase.

Each of the brethren must, in this phase of Court work, "screen cases and select for argument and select for decision only those which in our judgment," wrote a justice, "raise the most important and far-reaching questions."[54] This task is done, more or less arduously, by the justice and his or her staff. It is based, in some measure, on each justice's view of judicial role and on the scope of the powers of judicial review.

It is with respect to this individual phase of the Court's activities that Justice Powell's comment is so appropriate. "As much as 90 percent of our total time," he wrote, "we function as nine small, independent law firms."[55] In this activity, the role of the law clerk has increased dramatically. Powell and five others employed four law clerks, Chief Justice Burger used five, and Rehnquist and Stevens used three and two, respectively.[56]

During this period the Court does not hear oral argument or meet in Conference Session. Each justice "works largely in isolation, except as he chooses to seek consultation with others."[57] Some, such as Justice Brennan, for example, work the hallways quite a bit, while others, especially Justice Douglas, choose not to partake of that kind of lobbying.[58]

In the *Nixon* case, which did exhibit a high degree of intracourt consultation (even Douglas, as will be seen, participated in some informal discussions), in addition to the formal opinion writer, Burger, at least six justices wrote separate opinions or portions of opinions and circulated them to their colleagues: Powell, Douglas, Brennan, Stewart, Blackmun and White. A great deal of craftsmanship enters the development of a quality opinion; it is the expression of collegial thinking on a number of important issues.

In order to hold the majority, the drafter of the opinion has to be sure that it meets with the approval of the rest of the group. "Opinions for the Court," a scholar wrote, "are not statements of a particular justice's jurisprudence. Rather, they are negotiated documents forged from ideological divisions within the court."[59]

During this individual phase, communication takes place among the justices through drafts and the exchange of "Memorandum to the Conference" (MTTC) notes. Justice Blackmun, for example, wrote that

> A Memorandum to the Conference does have impact, for it sets forth in specific language the concerns entertained by the author. In some respect, this is better than general observations made orally at conference. And they tend to fill in the gap occasioned by the lack of time for extended conferences or one-on-one conversations. By a Memorandum . . . all nine are brought into the discussion. This is merely my own view; it may not coincide with the views of others.[60]

Additionally, the Court's process of arriving at decisions in cases does not give the justice the luxury of reflecting on a single case of importance to the exclusion of all others. Justices are reviewing and reflecting and writing on a number of cases simultaneously. For example, when the Court met in conference on July 23, 1974, the day before the *Nixon* opinion was announced, Burger's memo to the Conference had an attachment: the agenda for the Conference. In addition to the discussion of Nixon, four other circulating opinions were to be discussed (including the important busing case decided a day after *Nixon, Milliken v. Bradley*), two holds had to be discussed, and six petitions had to be acted upon.[61]

It is clear that "deciding the merits of those few cases taxes the individual powers of the justices and their capacity for compromise."[62] Examining the bargaining process among the justices during the last thirteen days of the Nixon negotiations clearly illustrates the fluidity of judicial choice. The process is a complex, time consuming one that demands intense commitment to the issues by the jurists contemplating the facts and the law.

It can also be a painful one. Justice Blackmun revealed a piece of advice about judicial opinion-writing given to him by Justice Black. "Harry," Black said, "never display agony in public in an opinion. Never display agony. Never say that this is an agonizing, difficult decision. Always write it as though it's clear as crystal."[63] Blackmun, however, was and remains an agonizer; he was not able to act on Black's advice.

The votes are tentative until an opinion announcing the Court's decision is handed down.[64] In *Nixon* Douglas was circulating his eighth draft of a separate concurring opinion just four days before the opinion was read in open court by the chief justice! Justice White, barely two days prior to the announcement, was informing (threatening) the chief that he would write a separate opinion if Burger did not change a portion of the executive privilege segment of the Burger draft opinion that was circulating.

That the Court moved so quickly on such an important constitutional case while it continued to review and resolve other important statutory and constitutional questions was a credit to the resolve of the justices. It was due in great part to their collective commitment to the belief, raised by Brennan in the first Conference Session on May 31, 1974, that it was the institution's "duty" to clarify the Watergate "mess." This clarification by the Court was not accomplished without difficulty.

POLITICS AND COURTS

Beyond doubt, the Watergate issue was the all-consuming political and moral dilemma of 1973–74. "The news about Watergate" wrote one scholar, "of course, had fully penetrated to Olympus. From the beginning, in fact, the justices had followed the unfolding scandal with increased fascination."[65] It is extraordinarily clear, in reviewing the papers of the justices, that they were very aware of the politics of the Watergate litigation and of the potential impact a definitive institutional judgment would have on the resolution of that dilemma. (Interestingly, Douglas, the justice whom Jaworski and Lacovara thought might write the opinion for the Court, initially believed that the motion for expedited Certiorari under Rule 20 should be denied because, in part, the issue was "political" and therefore nonjusticiable.) The Court's decision to bypass the Court of Appeals under the guidelines of Rule 20 was a "crucial" timing judgment.[66]

The Court's "headlong rush"[67] into the controversy was a critical factor in the resolution of the societal and constitutional crisis. The opinion of the court in *U.S. v. Nixon,* said one scholar, "represents nothing less than a bold and stunningly successful instance of judicial activism."[68] From Judge Sirica's perspective, the Court "would have delayed the cover-up trial perhaps into 1975 and would certainly have left the crippled president in office well beyond the time he was able to govern effectively"[69] had it not acted as quickly as it did. While there was some concern about expediting the case, thereby bypassing the Court of Appeals, the majority of the justices moved to expedite the litigation in order to, as Douglas wrote in his autobiography, "clarify the Watergate mess."[70]

The concern expressed by some of the justices in the May 31, 1974 Conference was reminiscent of the dissenting opinions in *U.S. v. New York Times and Washington Post* (1971), the *Pentagon Papers* case. Burger, Blackmun, and Harlan wrote dissenting opinions in that watershed First Amendment case that involved the Nixon administration's use of the judicial process to restrain freedom of the press. Their dissents reflected the view that "these cases have been conducted in unseemly haste. . . . Prompt judicial action does not mean unjudicial haste. . . . The court has been almost irresponsibly feverish in dealing with these cases."[71]

Burger's concern, voiced during the *Pentagon Papers* Conference Session was pervasive; it was voiced again and again in conference when he said that "no judge on any of the cases knows the whole facts." Until all the facts were in, Burger concluded, "He [was] unable to vote on the merits." Harlan, also in the Conference meeting, thought that the "judicial process has been made a travesty—it has been panicky and hurried . . . judicial review has been very, very limited."[72]

For some, then, indeed (as will be shown) for a *majority* of the brethren at the beginning of the fateful May 31, 1974, Conference Session, the Nixon case was litigation that begged for "judicial caution."[73] It was a caution occasioned by the organizational relationships between coordinate branches and by the traditional comity shown the federal courts of appeals by the Supreme Court.

There was also the cause for concern because the *Nixon* case, if taken (the Court, after all, could have allowed the court of appeals to render judgment and then not have granted certiorari), it would ultimately lead the brethren to raise, once again, some fundamental questions about constitutional principles. These issues, for example, separation of powers and the scope of judicial review, lay at the heart of the legal controversy surrounding the *Nixon* case. It was a controversy the justices of the Court were shortly to enter.

NOTES

1. Michael A. Genovese, "Richard M. Nixon and the Politicization of Justice," Paper Presented at the September 1987 American Political Science Association Annual Meetings, p. 25.

2. Quoted in *Congressional Quarterly Almanac* (Washington, D.C.: Congressional Quarterly Press, 1969), p. 130.

3. Gerald Gunther, "Judicial Hegemony and Legislative Autonomy," *UCLA Law Review*, 22, no.30 (1974), at 33.

4. Nixon quoted in Paul McCloskey, Jr., *Trust and Untruth: Political Deceit In America* (New York: Simon and Schuster, 1972), p. 189.

5. Genovese, "Richard M. Nixon," p. 26.

6. James F. Simon, *In His Own Image: The Supreme Court in Richard Nixon's America* (New York: David McKay and Co., 1974), p. 18.

7. See Bernard Schwartz's excellent book, *Packing The Court: The Conservative Campaign to Rewrite the Constitution* (New York: Charles Scribners Sons, 1988). It examines the Reagan administration's efforts to place on the federal bench men and women who shared the administration's political and social agenda.

8. See, generally, Richard Harris, *Decision* (New York: E. P. Dutton, 1971), for an excellent analysis of the Haynesworth-Carswell failed transactions.

9. See, generally, Bruce Allan Murphy, *Fortas: The Rise and Ruin of a Supreme Court Justice* (New York: William Morrow, 1988).

10. See, generally, Vincent Blasi, *The Burger Court* (New Haven: Yale University Press, 1984).

11. Paul A. Freund, "Forward: On Presidential Privilege," *Harvard Law Review* 88 (November 1974).

12. Burger quoted in Robert Woodward and Scott Armstrong, *The Brethren: Inside the Supreme Court* (Simon and Schuster, 1979), pp. 286–87.

13. See, generally, Howard Ball and Phillip Cooper, *Of Power and Right* (New York: Oxford University Press, 1990).

14. Woodward and Armstrong, *The Brethren*, p. 313.

15. Letter, William O. Douglas to Palmer Hoyt, May 3, 1973, Douglas Papers, Box 1659, Library of Congress (LC), Washington, D.C.

16. Letter, WOD to Roger Kent, February 4, 1974, Douglas Papers, Box 1659, LC.

17. See, generally, Chapter Thirteen in Ball and Cooper, *Of Power and Right*, for a review of the 1970 impeachment effort led by Ford against Douglas.

18. Warren Burger Interview with Bill Moyers, CBS-TV, 1987.

19. Bernard Schwartz, ed., *The Unpublished Opinions of the Burger Court* (New York: Oxford University Press, 1988), p. 5.

20. William O. Douglas, *The Court Years* (New York: Random House, 1980), p. 232.

21. Letter, WOD to Warren E. Burger, March 6, 1972, WODP LC, Washington, D. C.

22. Douglas wrote a letter to Justice Lewis Powell on March 8, 1972, in which the senior justice asked Powell "to put on paper the idea you expressed in Conference and I am sure you will get a majority." Letter, Douglas to Powell, WODP LC, Washington, D.C., *U.S. v. U.S. District Court*, 407 *U.S.* 297 (1972), involved a ruling of the Court invalidating Nixon's efforts to place wiretaps without a search warrant. There were three concurring opinions: Douglas, Burger, and White. Rehnquist did not participate in the discussion and in the final judgment.

23. *Lloyd Corp. v. Tanner*, 407 *U.S.* 551 (1972).

24. This procedural and substantive pattern of behavior went back to the chief justiceship tenure of Roger B. Taney. See, for example, Schwartz, *Unpublished Opinions of the Burger Court*, p. 8.

25. Letter, Douglas to Burger, May 1, 1972, WODP LC, Washington, D.C.

26. Interview, Warren E. Burger, December 21, 1987, Washington D.C.

27. Douglas quoted in James Simon, *An Independent Journey: The Life of William O. Douglas* (New York: Harper and Row, 1980), p. 14.

28. Schwartz, ed., *Unpublished Opinions of the Burger Court*, p. 10.

29. Woodward and Armstrong, *Brethren*, p. 289.

30. James Clayton, *The Making of Justice: The Supreme Court in Action* (New York: E. P. Dutton, 1964), p. 217.

31. Woodward and Armstrong, *The Brethren*, p. 290.

32. Blackmun quoted in *New York Times*, March 8, 1986, p. 7.

33. *Roe v. Wade*, 410 *U.S.* 113 (1973).
34. *Sierra Club v. Morton*, 405 *U.S.* 727 (1972).
35. Quoted in Congressional Quarterly, *Watergate: Chronology of a Crisis* (Washington, D.C.: Congressional Quarterly Press, 1975), p. 257.
36. Quoted in Schwartz, ed., *Unpublished Opinions of the Burger Court*, p. 12.
37. Woodward and Armstrong, *The Brethren*, p. 290.
38. Generally, see Robert Woodward and Carl Bernstein, *Final Days* (New York: Simon and Schuster, 1974).
39. Ibid., p. 262.
40. Ibid.
41. Quoted in O'Brien, *Storm Center: The Supreme Court in American Politics* (New York: W. W. Norton, 1986), p. 214.
42. Bernard Schwartz, ed., *The Unpublished Opinions of the Warren Court* (New York: Oxford University Press, 1987), p. 7.
43. William J. Brennan, "Inside View of the High Court," *New York Times Sunday Magazine*, October 6, 1963.
44. Quoted in Tom C. Clark, "The Internal Operations of the U.S. Supreme Court," *Judicature* 43 (1959): 48.
45. See David Danielski, "The Influence of the Chief Justice in the Decisional Process," paper delivered at the American Political Science Association Annual Meeting, New York, September 1960.
46. For example, after some essays appeared that discussed the Supreme Court's decision in *Brown v. Board*, based in part on the conference notes of Justice Harold Burton, Justice Hugo Black became so incensed at the use made of such data that he instructed his son, Hugo, Jr., to burn all his conference notes after his death. On the other hand, Justices Douglas and Brennan, among many justices, have left all their papers and, in Brennan's case, is allowing a few scholars to examine docket books and conference notes that were written by him.
47. Loren Beth, *Politics, the Constitution and the Supreme Court* (New York: Row, Peterson, 1962), p. 41.
48. Letter, Hugo L. Black to Howard Ball, January 31, 1969.
49. Letter, William Rehnquist to Robert Bradley, in *Law, Courts, and Judicial Process Section Newsletter*, 7, no.1 (Fall, 1989): 8. In another letter written by Henry J. Abraham, he quoted Justice Sandra Day O'Connor on this matter: "The Chief Justice now speaks and votes first, and the Junior Justice speaks and votes last." Ibid., p. 9.
50. J. Woodford Howard, "On the Fluidity of Judicial Choice," *American Political Science Review* 62 (March 1968): 43.
51. Personal communication, Hugo Black to Howard Ball, January 21, 1969.

52. William J. Brennan, "Inside View of the High Court," *New York Times Sunday Magazine*, October 6, 1963, p. 22.

53. Letter, Hugo Black to Howard Ball, January 21, 1969.

54. Brennan, "Inside View."

55. Lewis R. Powell, "What The Justices Are Saying," *American Bar Association Journal* 62 (1981): 1454.

56. Mark W. Cannon and David O'Brien, *Views From The Bench* (Chatham, NJ: Chatham House, 1985), p. 52.

57. Stephen Early, *Constitutional Courts of the United States* (Totawa, NJ: Littlefield, Adams, 1975), p. 36.

58. Douglas often told his wife, Catherine, and others, that he "had one soul to save, his own." See, generally, Howard Ball and Phillip Cooper, *Of Power and Right: Justices Black and Douglas* (New York: Oxford University Press, 1990).

59. O'Brien, *Storm Center*, p. 213.

60. Letter, Harry A. Blackmun to Howard Ball, November 26, 1986.

61. Memo to the Conference (MTTC), July 23, 1974, Brennan Papers, Box 329, LC, Washington, D.C.

62. O'Brien, *Storm Center*, p. 213.

63. David Rhode, "Policy Goals and Opinion Coalitions in the Supreme Court," *Midwest Journal of Political Science* 26 (May 1972).

64. Howard Ball, *Courts and Politics* 2d ed. (Englewood Cliffs, NJ: Prentice-Hall, 1987), p. 215.

65. Bernard Schwartz, ed., *The Unpublished Opinions of the Burger Court*, p. 155.

66. Blasi, *Burger Court*, p. 200.

67. Ibid.

68. Ibid., p. 201.

69. John J. Sirica, *To Set the Record Straight* (New York: Norton, 1979), pp. 224–25.

70. Douglas, *The Court Years*, p. 202.

71. 403 *U.S.* 713 (1971).

72. Douglas Conference Notes, June 26, 1971, Douglas Papers, Box 1519, LC.

73. Robert F. Nagel, "The Legislative Veto, The Constitution and the Courts," *Constitutional Commentaries* 2, no.61 (1986), at 65.

4

The Critical Issues: Separation of Powers, Executive Privilege, and Judicial Review (Revisited)

What troubled the justices, in addition to the gory public spectacle of a political scandal that led directly to the White House, was the hard realization that the Court was being dragged into the very core of a set of critical and conflicting constitutional debates argued by the counsel for opposing parties.

From the very first days following the revelation that Nixon had taped conversations to the days preceding the oral arguments before the justices in Court, the lawyers for the president argued that the concept of separation of powers inherent in the Constitution conferred an absolute immunity on the president with regard to private discussions he may have had with aides and assistants in the White House. Conversations between the president and aides were confidential; furthermore, the doctrine of separation of powers precluded any judicial review of his claim. Before the Supreme Court, Nixon's lawyers argued that the White House "claim[s an] absolute executive privilege against inquiry by the coordinate Judicial Branch" into such matters.[1]

The president did not have to turn over the tapes to the judicial branch, Nixon's attorneys claimed, unless he wished to do so. In any event, the federal judges were absolutely—categorically—barred from reviewing his actions because of the separation of powers concept.

For the special prosecutor and his counsel, there was no constitutional basis to the Nixon executive privilege claim; federal courts were empowered to review the actions of the president in the matter involving a special prosecutor's activities. Furthermore, the separation of powers concept was never envisioned as an absolute bar against judicial review unless a matter was determined to be non-justiciable by the federal judges themselves.

Clearly, then, *United States v. Nixon* raised anew the question of the meaning and the scope of the concept of separation of powers through the very specific theme of executive privilege. In that manner, the *Nixon* litigation raised, once again, the question of the scope of judicial review in a constitutional system.

SEPARATION OF POWERS

The separation of powers doctrine "deals with the relations among institutions of American government."[2] The value was implicitly[3] adopted in 1787

> not to promote efficiency but to preclude the exercise of arbitrary power. The purpose was, not to avoid friction, but, by means of the inevitable friction incident to the distribution of governmental powers among three departments, to save the people from autocracy.[4]

The men who wrote the 1787 Constitution were committed to the ideals, occasionally in conflict, of greater efficiency in government as well as the prevention of tyranny.[5] Therefore they thought it wise to try to divide governing power between the national legislature, the executive and the judiciary. The concept was adopted by the framers in order to reduce, not necessarily eliminate, the risk of oppression.[6] They were men of the enlightenment, they were realists.

While the Constitution contains no specific "separation" language, the concept is implicit in the distribution of powers among the three coordinate national branches. Articles I, II, and III separate powers,[7] and from this separation

> is derived the doctrine that certain functions, because of their essential nature, may properly be exercised by only a particular branch of the government; that such functions cannot be delegated to any other branch; and that one department may not interfere with another by usurping its powers or by supervising their exercise.[8]

So, according to one scholar, the separation of powers can be described conceptually and formalistically as follows:

> congress legislates, and it only legislates; the President sees to the faithful execution of those laws and, in the domestic context at least, that is all he does; the courts decide specific cases of law-application, and that is their sole function. These three powers of government are kept radically separate, because if the same body exercised all three of them, or even two, it might no longer be possible to keep it within the constraints of law.[9]

If these descriptions were the reality of separation of powers, then and now, if there was only such a rigid *application* of the separation of powers concept, then the presidential argument made in the 1973–1974 *Nixon* legal briefs would have been a potent one.

However, historically, the separation of powers doctrine has been viewed and interpreted—by congresses, presidential administrations and federal judges—in a much more flexible manner. Even in 1787, according to some scholars, there was no "coherent and generally shared view of separation of powers."[10] Some go so far as to argue that there was not a doctrine of separation of powers that was even implicitly incorporated into the Constitution.[11]

Justice Robert H. Jackson offered a realistic, contemporary view of the separation of powers concept in his concurring opinion in the watershed 1952 "steel seizure" case:

> While the Constitution diffuses power the better to secure liberty, it also contemplates that practice will integrate the dispersed powers into

a workable government. It enjoins upon its branches separateness but interdependence, autonomy but reciprocity.[12]

Throughout America's political history, presidents have worked with congressional leaders to attack major problems that beset the society. Federal courts have accepted and constitutionalized the creation of the major hybrid of the American political system in the twentieth century, the federal regulatory agencies—often referred to as the fourth branch of government. Federal courts have, for the most part, crafted opinions to legitimatize (through statutory interpretation) the controversial actions of the coordinate agencies of the national government.

Given the reality of intergovernmental relations at the national level, a very formalistic separation of powers is a "misnomer. No precise line is or could be drawn between the three branches of the national government."[13] More importantly, relative to a meaningful definition of separation of powers, interaction, *not* independence, has characterized the relationship between the coordinate branches.[14]

Each of the three coordinate agencies of national government has a set of powers, defined in various ways (specifically or very broadly) in the first three Articles of the Constitution.[15] However, in order to make government work more responsibly, there has emerged the interactive relationship between Congress, president and judiciary.

EXECUTIVE PRIVILEGE

The *Nixon* litigation raised the question of the scope and the meaning of the separation of powers concept. It did so very directly by focussing on the meaning of executive privilege. The counsel for the president claimed that there is an *inherent* constitutional power for him to treat (or not to treat, as the case may be) as absolutely confidential any communications he or she has with subordinates in the executive branch. The term itself is one of recent vintage, having been coined by the Court in a 1953 case, *United States v. Reynolds*.[16]

Like other constitutional values, the concept as such is nowhere to be found in the Constitution itself. The position on "executive privilege" taken by President Nixon and his legal staff was a fundamental, absolutist one: The President and only the President, has the absolute power, consistent with the doctrine of separation of powers, to decide what documents or other information should be released to either of the other coordinate branches of government. Using the rigid, nonflexible concept of separation of powers as the legal foundational premise, Nixon's lawyers maintained that the concept prohibited congressional committees or federal courts from telling the president what he must do with documents and other forms of communications in the executive branch.

As Cox noted, "the controversy over executive privilege arises from our constitutional separation of government into coordinate legislative, executive, and judicial branches."[17] President Nixon's argument that—because of his lawyers' acceptance of the formalistic notion of separation of powers, he had the sole and absolute power to determine what information would be released—had never been established by the Supreme Court.[18] He claimed that because the clash he was having with Special Prosecutor Leon Jaworski over the release of sixty-four tapes was an intrabranch dispute, it was therefore a clash "which the President, not the Courts, has the [sole] authority to resolve."[19]

In a scathing attack, in *Executive Privilege: A Constitutional Myth,*[20] Raoul Berger took issue with Nixon's view of the derivative right of executive privilege he claimed as being an inherent part of the executive power. For Berger, the concept of executive privilege "is a myth, . . . the origins of which are lost in the mists of antiquity."[21] Directly countering the president's assertion that the separation of powers doctrine is the foundation for executive privilege, Berger noted that "such reliance overlooks Montesquieu's unqualified statement that the legislature has the *right* to examine how 'its laws have been executed' " (original emphasis).[22] For Berger, in the final analysis, "executive privilege needs to be lifted from the field of legal esoterica and viewed in terms of underlying reality; *as a shield for presidential unaccountability*" (emphasis added).[23]

The 1973–74 litigation in the federal courts, *Nixon v. Sirica*[24] and *U.S. v. Nixon,*[25] examined that question of executive privilege as well as the broader doctrine of separation of powers. For the first time, the Supreme Court passed "on the question of executive privilege for confidential communications to which the president is a party."[26] Analyzing the question of executive privilege and separation of powers meant that the justices of the Court had to acknowledge the proactive character of judicial review.

INTERPRETIVE JUDICIAL REVIEW

As noted earlier, a major precaution against governmental tyranny is the American judiciary's power of judicial review. Judicial interpretation of the Constitution and judicial examination of how *others* have interpreted the Constitution involves that uniquely American judicial power. As was noted earlier, "the problem of access to the federal courts is a problem in the separation of powers."[27] Federal judges, especially the justices of the U.S. Supreme Court, will serve as liberal or conservative gatekeepers based on their views of separation of powers as well as their views of the role and function of the Court in the political process.

While Justices Felix Frankfurter, John M. Harlan, II, and William Rehnquist were very concerned about the consequences if the federal courts were to become enmeshed in the political thicket, Justices William O. Douglas, William J. Brennan and Thurgood Marshall did not share the somewhat paralyzing fears held by their more conservative brethren. They viewed the federal courts, especially the Supreme Court, as a major participant in the policy process and, as such, had a proactive role to play.

In one sense, Frankfurter, Harlan, and Rehnquist shared one view of judicial review whereas Douglas, Brennan, and Marshall acted on the basis of another conception. If the Constitution is itself two complex sets of value judgments about the nature of power and the inherent limits on power in a constitutional republic,[28] then judicial review can be seen as either an *interpretive* (Frankfurter/Harlan/Rehnquist) or a *noninterpretive* (Douglas/Brennan/Thurgood Marshall) review, by the courts, of the Constitution and the values associated with the document.

Interpretive review is that re-examination of the values in the Constitution by federal judges, especially the justices of the U.S. Supreme Court. What, for example, is the meaning and the scope of the Commerce Clause, war power, and the relationship of a president to his subordinates in the executive branch? Through the mechanism of the ripe case or controversy before the Court, in which the parties address such issues, a judge will engage in interpretive judicial review to try to resolve the issue. But the judge is constrained in such an activity by the words of the Constitution and/or by the intent of the framers.

The Court engages in interpretive judicial review "when it ascertains the constitutionality of a given policy choice by reference to one of the value judgments of which the Constitution consists—that is, by a value judgment embodied, though not necessarily explicitly, either in some particular provision of the text of the Constitution or in the overall structure of government ordained by the Constitution."[29]

To some, this kind of judicial review is a conservative effort, justified by scholars such as Robert Bork[30] and Raoul Berger[31], meant to "constrain the judiciary sufficiently to prevent judicial tyranny."[32] Judges are constrained, when using the interpretive judicial review concept, because they "must look both to the words of the document and, because such words as 'equal protection' and 'due process of law' are too opaque, to the intent of those who wrote the document."[33]

For example, in a 1984 lecture, Bork said that the "moral content of law must be given by the morality of the framer or the legislator, never by the morality of the judge." For Bork, the judge's sole task was to transfer the morality of the legislator or framer "into a rule to govern unforseen circumstances." As for the proper morality of the federal judges, Bork's response was forthright: "Abstinance from giving his own desires free play, . . . [the] continuing self-conscious renunciation of power."[34] Clearly, Judge Bork is insistent on restricting the power of the Court "in the name of liberty," whereas his opponents, the legal liberals on and off the Court want to "augment judicial power in the name of social justice."[35]

Noninterpretive review, on the other hand, is that review by judges of cases and controversies (for example, judicial examination of the constitutionality of an anti-abortion statute) in which the jurist resolves the litigation by reference to a value other than one that has been "constitutionalized" by those who wrote the Constitution or who added the Amendments to it. Judges engage in this contemporary extraconstitutional judicial review when they make "the determination of constitutionality by reference to a value judgment other than one constitutionalized by the framers."[36] Obviously, for Court watchers such as Bork, this type of judicial behavior gives the judge's "desires free play" and leads to the creation of new, extraconstitutional values. As Bork wrote, federal judges are beholden to legislative majorities when the Constitution is silent on an issue." Being 'at the mercy of legislative majorities' is merely another way of describing the basic American plan: representative democracy. We may all deplore its results from time to time, but that does not empower judges to set them aside; the Constitution allows only voters to do that."[37]

Clearly, in the *Nixon* litigation the justices of the Supreme Court, as well as all the other federal judges involved in the earlier litigation associated with the Watergate matter,[38] were for the most part engaged in interpretive judicial review of the implicit and flexible concept of separation of powers. This did not minimize the extent of the controversy that surrounded the discussion of the constitutional values of separation of powers.

However, there were three justices who believed, to varying degrees, that the Court was engaged in noninterpretive judicial review when it examined and *incorporated* the concept of presidential privilege into the Constitution's Article II, in *Nixon*. They were of the opinion that the concept of presidential privilege was not to be found in the Constitution and that the Court majority was creating an inherent power of the presidency where none had existed. What is truly ironic is that two of these jurists, Justices William O. Douglas and William J. Brennan, were very creative noninterpretive judicial review activists.[39] The next three chapters examine the discussions that took place in the Court on these issues of procedure and substance.

NOTES

1. See, for example, *Nixon v. Administrator of General Services*, 433 *U.S.* 425 (1975), at 447. Nixon's Attorney General, Richard G. Kliendeinst, argued that Nixon was "empowered to forbid federal employees from testifying before congressional committees under any circumstances and to block congressional demands for any document within the executive branch." Quoted in Raoul Berger, *Executive Privilege: A Constitutional Myth* (New York: New American Library, 1974), pp.254–55.

2. John H. Garvey and T. Alexander Aleinikoff, *Modern Constitutional Theory: A Reader* (St. Paul: West Publishing Company, 1988), p. 178.

3. "If the Framers decided to incorporate a requirement of separation of powers in the Constitution, that decision was implicit rather than explicit." Richard J. Pierce, Jr., "Morrison v. Olson: Separation of Powers and the Structure of Government," in *1988-The Supreme Court Review*, ed. Philip B. Kurland, et al. (Chicago: University of Chicago Press, 1988), p. 10.

4. Louis Brandeis, dissenting, *Myers v. United States*, 272 *U.S.* 52 (1926), at 293.

5. See James Madison, Alexander Hamilton, and John Jay, *The Federalist Papers*, ed. Isaac Kramnick (New York: Penguin Books, 1987) 47, 51. In *Federalist* 47, Madison responded to critics of the Constitution who had objected to what they believed was the absence of a separation of powers, which Madison labelled an "essential precaution in favor of liberty." He wrote that "no political truth is certainly of greater intrinsic value, or is stamped with the authority of more enlightened patrons of liberty, than that on which the objection is founded. The accumulation of all powers, legislative, executive and judiciary, in the same hands, whether of one, a few, or many, and whether hereditary, self-appointed, or elective may justly be pronounced the very definition of tyranny."

In *Federalist* 51, Madison wrote: "But the great security against a gradual concentration of the several powers in the same department, consists in giving to those who administer each department the necessary constitutional means and personal motives to resist encroachments of the others. The provision for defense must in this, as in all other cases, be made commensurate to the danger of attack. Ambition must be made to counteract ambition."

But, in *Federalist* 48, Madison discussed the separation of powers concept in a very different manner. "It is agreed on all sides that the powers properly belonging to one department ought not to be *directly* and *completely* administered by the other departments" (my emphasis). See also *Federalist* 65, 75 and 81.

"However," as a contemporary historian of the Constitution has written, the principle of separation of powers was "by no means as simple and self-evident as the Federalists suggested. The seemingly rational division of government into three separate functions . . . carried with it historically in the British world and even theoretically in the writings of both Locke and Montesquieu, the notion not only of separation but of mixture, too" (*Federalist*, p. 48).

6. Tushnet, "Following the Rules Laid Down: A Critique of Interpretivism and Neutral Principles," *Harvard Law Review*, 96 no.4 (February 1983): 784.

7. Article I: "All legislative powers herein granted shall be vested in a Congress of the United States." Article II: "The executive power shall be vested in a President of the United States." Article III: "The judicial power shall be vested in one Supreme Court and in such inferior courts as the congress shall . . . ordain and establish."

8. Alpheus T. Mason and Donald G. Stephenson, Jr., *American Constitutional Law* (Englewood Cliffs, NJ: Prentice Hall, 1990), p. 71.

9. Peter L. Strauss, "The Place of Agencies in Government: The Separation of Powers and the Fourth Branch," *Columbia Law Review*, 84, no.573 (1984): at 577. "For the safety of the citizenry from tyrannous government these three functions must be kept in distinct places." Justice Antonin Scalia, in his dissent in *Morrison v. Olson*, 108 *S Ct* 2597 (1988), argued for such a rigid separation of powers. For Scalia, the independent counsel's activities under the Ethics in Government Act are totally executive because that function has "always and everywhere" been an activity of persons in the executive branch of government. Article II, for Scalia, "does not mean some of the executive power, but all of the executive power." Because the Act removes some of the president's responsibility over the independent counsel, it is an unconstitutional violation of the separation of powers concept (at 2626).

10. Gerhard Casper, "An Essay On Separation of Powers: Some Early Versions and Practices," *William and Mary Law Review*, 30 (1989): 220.

11. Ibid., p. 224; Neil McDonald, *Novos Ordo Seclorum: The Intellectual Origins of the Constitution* (Kansas City: University of Kansas Press, 1985).

12. Jackson, concurring, *Youngstown Sheet and Tube Company v. Sawyer*, 343 *U.S.* 579 (1952), at 635. Pierce writes that the "Framers evidenced a dedication to careful blending of powers to achieve coor-

dination in the exercise of a wide variety of functions that defied easy configuration." *Morrison v. Olson*, pp. 8–9.

13. Mason and Stephenson, *American Constitutional Law*, p. 72.

14. See, generally, Archibald Cox, "Executive Privilege," *University of Pennsylvania Law Review* 122, no.1383 (1974).

15. There are also distinct sets of limits on the use of these powers in the Articles themselves, in the application of the general concept of Checks and Balances, in the Bill of Rights, and in judicial review, a practice that Madison referred to as the society's auxiliary precaution against tyranny.

16. 345 *U.S.* 1 (1953).

17. Cox, "Executive Privilege," p. 1384.

18. The 1807 Burr trial, in a federal court with Chief Justice John Marshall sitting as circuit judge, did establish certain principles regarding the relationship between the executive and judicial branches on matters of executive privilege, but these were not binding precedent in the *Nixon* litigation. See Paul A. Freund, "Foreword: On Presidential Privilege," *Harvard Law Review*, 88 (November 1974): 30–31 for an examination of these guidelines.

19. Freund, "Foreword: On Presidential Privilege," 15.

20. (Cambridge: Harvard University Press, 1974).

21. Ibid., p. 1.

22. Ibid., p. 12.

23. Ibid., p. 416.

24. *Nixon v. Sirica* 487 *F 2d* 700 (D.C. Circuit, 1973).

25. *United States v. Nixon* 418 *U.S.* 683 (1974).

26. Freund, "Foreword: On Presidential Privilege," 13.

27. Wallace Mendelson, "Mr. Justice Douglas and Government By Judiciary," *Journal of Politics*, 38 (1976): 937.

28. "The Constitution consists of a complex of value judgments constitutionalized by the framers." Michael J. Perry, *The Constitution, The Courts, and Human Rights: An Inquiry Into the Legitimacy of Constitutional Policymaking By the Judiciary* (New Haven: Yale University Press, 1982), p. 38.

29. Ibid., p. 10.

30. Robert Bork, *The Tempting of America: The Political Seduction of the Law* (New York: Free Press, 1989).

31. See Raoul Berger, *Government by Judiciary* (Cambridge: Harvard University Press, 1977).

32. Mark V. Tushnet, "Following The Rules Laid Down," no.4, p. 785.

33. Ibid., p. 786. This is, for Tushnet, the classic example of the

"dead hand of the past" determining judicial behavior. Interpretivism "requires that judges today be able to trace historical continuities between the institutions the framers knew and those that contemporary judges know. . . . [The concept] attempts to implement the rule of law by assuming that the meaning of words and rules are stable over extended periods." pp. 824, 785.

34. Quoted in Elder Witt, *A Different Justice: Reagan and The Supreme Court* (Washington, D.C.: Congressional Quarterly Press, 1986), p. 149.

35. John P. Diggins, "The Judge Pleads His Case," *New York Times Book Review*, November 19, 1989, p. 15.

36. Perry, *The Constitution, The Courts and Human Rights*, p. 11. For scholars, noninterpretive judicial review occurs when the Court "reaches a decision without really interpreting any provision of the constitutional text—although, to be sure, the Court may explain its decision with rhetoric designed to create the illusion that it is merely 'interpreting' or 'applying' some constitutional provision" (at 11).

37. Bork, *Tempting of Justice*, p. 49.

38. See *Nixon v. Sirica* 487 *F 2d* 700 (1973).

39. For example, see their views of the right of privacy in *Griswold v. Connecticut* 381 *U.S.* 479 (1965), Douglas for the majority, and in *Eisenstadt v. Baird* 405 *U.S.* 438 (1972), Brennan for the majority. Douglas wrote in *Griswold* that various protections found in the Bill of Rights "have penumbras, formed by emanations from those guarantees that help give them life and substance. Various guarantees create zones of privacy." For Brennan, the core privacy issue in *Eisenstadt* involved basic freedoms related to one's individual liberty, including "freedom from bodily restraint, freedom to do with one's body as one likes, and a freedom to care for one's health."

5

U.S. v. Nixon, I: The Duty to Hear the Case

On March 1, 1974, H. R. Haldeman, John Mitchell, John Ehrlichman, Gordon Strachan, Robert Mardian, Kenneth Parkinson, and Charles Colson were indicted by a federal Grand Jury. The special prosecutor's office had the burden of developing the case for the forthcoming criminal trial, *U.S. v. Mitchell, et al.* (scheduled for September 9, 1974) and requested that the federal court issue a subpoena to the president of the United States for the additional evidence needed for the trial. If issued, it would direct Nixon to produce tape recordings and documents relating to sixty-four conversations between Nixon and advisors. On April 18, Judge John Sirica issued the subpoena *duces tecum* pursuant to Rule 17c of the Federal Rules of Criminal Procedure.

On May 1, 1974, James St. Clair, the president's newly appointed counsel, filed a Special Appearance and motion to quash the subpoena. He argued that the materials sought "are within the constitutional privilege of the president to refuse to disclose confidential information when disclosure would be contrary to the public interest."[1] In addition to moving to quash the subpoena, based on this formal claim of executive privilege, St. Clair argued that the issue was an internal controversy not subject to judicial scrutiny. (He also moved on May 11 for an order of the court to expunge the Grand Jury's naming of Nixon as an unindicted co-conspirator in the upcoming criminal trial.)

On May 20, Sirica denied both motions and ordered Nixon to produce the sixty-four tapes. The federal judge found that Jaworski met the requirements of Rule 17c and that the prosecutors' submissions constituted a prima facie showing adequate to rebut the confidentiality privilege claim raised by the president. Four days later St. Clair filed notice of appeal in the U.S. District Court and docketed the appeal in the Court of Appeals of the District of Columbia Circuit.

FILING THE EXPEDITED PETITION IN THE SUPREME COURT

Jaworski that same day then did an "extraordinary"[2] thing. He took the "drastic step"[3] of requesting a writ of certiorari from the U.S. Supreme Court before judgment of the Court of Appeals. The request for bypass of the Court of Appeals route to the Supreme Court was an extremely rare path. In almost 200 years, only six such expedited cases had actually come before the Court from the federal district court, the last one being the 1952 "Steel Seizure" case[4]—twenty-two years earlier. Furthermore, the expedited request needs an affirmative vote of five justices, not the typical vote of four needed to grant certiorari.

Jaworski petitioned the Court, arguing that without the Court of Appeals bypass, the trial scheduled for September 9 would have to be delayed by many months and that

> the issues involved were of grave national importance; and the Court of Appeals had essentially ruled on the relevant legal issues in *Nixon v. Sirica*. The President, in response, suggested that the expedited procedure would unnecessarily pressure the Court and the parties and inevitably lead to a hastily prepared decision.[5]

Phillip Lacovara, Jaworski's young chief counsel, recently commented that the special prosecutor's staff had a

> reasonable degree of confidence that we could get a 5:3 decision [a one-vote margin], but that even a 5:3 would have left the president with some elbow room to claim that he was not beholden to the Court . . . on this delicate issue of executive privilege [because there was not a definitive judgment by the Court].[6]

They really did not expect to see the 8:0 opinion created by the Supreme Court in the *Nixon* litigation.

He also described some of the strategies employed by the Jaworski forces to assist them in their effort to win a tough suit against a sitting president. The special prosecutors tried to

> analogize the special prosecutor to the official the Court was accustomed to seeing represent the United States in its sovereign capacity, namely, the [U.S.] Solicitor General. We had our briefs printed in the same extraordinary and unique color that only the solicitor general uses. Nixon wound up using a color, because of our preemption, that a private party would be using.[7]

Jaworski and Lacovara attempted to "shape the controversy not as a separation of powers dispute but rather as a garden-variety controversy between the United States and a person [Nixon] who had relevant and important evidence."[8] Ironically, they succeeded more than they liked in shifting the attention of the Court away from the seriousness of the constitutional arguments surrounding the separation of powers and executive privilege.[9]

The day after Jaworski's sudden and surprising filing of the bypass petition, Chief Justice Burger, after a conversation with Justices Stewart and Powell, wrote a note to his colleagues. While he was concerned about the Court being "pressured or rushed by news media or anyone else, nevertheless, the case is one of obvious importance and time factors are important." He indicated that he would "canvass all the members of the Court to secure reactions with the idea of having the Clerk call Mr. St. Clair and suggest that the Court would like to have his response if at all possible by next Thursday . . . so as to enable the court to begin its consideration of the petition."[10] A conference was set for May 31 in order for the Supreme Court to respond to Jaworski's petition and the president's response.

Three days before the scheduled Conference, Justice Rehnquist wrote to Burger. While Rehnquist believed in "having a full court decide important issues of constitutional law," he regretted that he "must disqualify [him]self from participation." His decision was not based on his "previous relationship with the named parties in the case before us," but because "this litigation" is an "offshoot of *U.S. v. Mitchell*. . . ." Because of his "varying degrees of close professional association with three of the named defendants in that action . . . , it seems to me that there is no doubt as to my proper course."[11] (see exhibit 5.1).

On May 30, a day before the conference, James B. Gingy, clerk of the Court, prepared and circulated at Burger's request a detailed nine-page Memorandum for the Conference. It framed (see exhibit 5.2) six threshold issues for the eight jurists:

1. Did Jaworski have standing to seek a petition for certiorari before judgment under Rule 20?
2. Did Jaworski, as an "agent" of the Executive Branch, have the authority to conduct and argue a case before the Court?
3. Could Judge Sirica's order be appealed?
4. How had the phrase "imperative public importance" in Rule 20 been interpreted by the Court?
5. Did the district court apply Rule 17c of the Federal Rules/Criminal Procedure (FRCP) correctly? Was executive privilege a nonreviewable assertion of presidential power, or could the district court interpose and make judgment on that constitutional question?
6. Was the Court of Appeals's decision in *Nixon v. Sirica* (1973) a controlling decision regarding the question of executive privilege?

This very timely memo framed the conference discussion. Inexorably, these questions led to the overarching substantive question associated with the separation of powers concept: executive privilege.

THE SUPREME COURT'S MAY 31, 1974, CONFERENCE SESSION: THE CRITICAL DECISION

On May 31 the eight justices met in conference to review the petition for an expedited writ of certiorari. Interestingly, the

Exhibit 5.1
Personal Correspondence from Justice Rehnquist to Chief Justice Burger

Supreme Court of the United States
Washington, D. C. 20543

CHAMBERS OF
JUSTICE WILLIAM H. REHNQUIST

May 28, 1974

Re: <u>No. 73-1766 - U.S. v. Nixon</u>

Dear Chief:

I have publicly said since coming to the Court that there is a strong policy in favor of having a full Court decide important questions of constitutional law. If importance may be judged by the amount of public attention focused on a case, this one is surely important. Therefore it is a matter of regret to me that I feel I must disqualify myself from participation.

While I would not disqualify myself because of any previous relationship with the named parties in the case before us, the petition makes clear that this discovery litigation is an offshoot of <u>U.S.</u> v. <u>Mitchell</u>, a pending criminal prosecution in the District Court. I had varying degrees of close professional association with three of the named defendants in that action, each of whom could stand to gain or lose as a result of the outcome of this Court's decision regarding discovery. It therefore seems to me that there is no doubt as to my proper course, and I have advised Mike Rodak accordingly.

Sincerely,

WHR

The Chief Justice

Copies to the Conference

initial vote whether to grant certiorari, based on a review of the Brennan and Douglas docket files, was a strongly negative one. Evidently, the brethren had entered the Conference Session with the attitude that the Court *ought not* to enter this very obvious political thicket.

According to Justice Brennan's records, he and Thurgood Marshall were the only early supporters of an expedited certiorari grant by the Court. From the notes taken at the conference, it is abundantly clear that Justices Blackmun, White, Powell, Stewart, Douglas, and Burger were not inclined to hear the *Nixon*

Exhibit 5.2
Memorandum to the Conference, Prepared by James B. Gingy at Chief Justice Burger's Request

Supreme Court of the United States
Washington, D. C. 20543

CHAMBERS OF
THE CHIEF JUSTICE

May 30, 1974

Re: 73-1766 - U. S. v. Nixon

MEMORANDUM TO THE CONFERENCE:

Enclosed is Mr. Ginty's memo which has just reached my desk. As soon as the response comes in, it will be circulated to each of you. I have asked him to prepare a memo on the response if time permits.

Regards,

WEB

Supreme Court of the United States
Washington, D. C. 20543

May 30, 1974

MEMORANDUM TO THE CONFERENCE

Subject: United States v. Nixon, 73-1766 (Petition for Writ of Certiorari to CA (D. C.) before Judgment)

This memorandum is submitted at the request of the Chief Justice.

FACTS: Pursuant to Rule 17(c), Fed. R. Crim. P., the Special Prosecutor moved in the District Court for issuance of a subpoena commanding the President to produce certain specified materials in the case of United States v. Mitchell, et al. Three defendants, Colson, Mardian and Strachan, joined in the Special Prosecutor's motion. Relying on the legal memorandum and affidavit of the Special Prosecutor in support of the motion, the District Court (Sirica) ordered that the subpoena issue, commanding production for *in camera* inspection by the Court.

Prior to the return date of the subpoena, the President entered a special appearance and filed a motion to quash the subpoena. The motion included a formal claim of privilege. The Special Prosecutor and certain of the Mitchell defendants filed papers opposing the President's motion to quash. Defendant Strachan also filed a motion for issuance of a subpoena identical to that of the Special Prosecutor in the event that enforcement of the Special Prosecutor's subpoena is abandoned. The Special Prosecutor's submission, containing a lengthy and detailed showing of its need for the subpoenaed items and their relevance, has been placed under seal. Argument was made *in camera*.

In entering a special appearance, the President contended that the District Court lacked jurisdiction to enforce the subpoena on the grounds that (1) the courts are without authority to rule on the scope or applicability of executive privilege when asserted by the President and (2) the dispute between the President and the Special Prosecutor regarding the production of evidence is an intra-branch controversy wholly within the jurisdiction of the executive branch to resolve. The District Court found that the first argument was decided in

Nixon v. Sirica, 487 F. 2d 700 (D. C. Cir. 1973), and that the second had no application to the present situation in view of the Special Prosecutor's independence and delegation of full authority, inter alia, to contest the assertion of Executive privilege.

With respect to the motion to quash, the District Court dismissed the President's two principal arguments finding (1) that the Special Prosecutor met the requirements of Rule 17(c) and (2) that the Special Prosecutor's submissions constitute a prima facie showing adequate to rebut the confidentiality privilege interposed by the President, and a demonstration of need sufficiently compelling to warrant judicial examination in chambers incident to weighing claims of privilege. The District Court did not reach the President's third argument which spoke to the defendants' contention that the subpoenaed materials are producible to them under Brady v. Maryland, 373 U.S. 83 (1963), the Jencks Act, 18 U.S.C. 3500 and the discovery rules for criminal proceedings.

The District Court ordered that the subpoenaed documents be delivered to the Court, but provided that should the President seek review in the Court of Appeals, the order shall be stayed pending the completion of such review.

On May 24, the President filed a notice of appeal from the District Court's order, and the certified record from the District Court was docketed in the Court of Appeals (D. C.). The President also filed a petition for a writ of mandamus in the Court of Appeals seeking review of the District Court's order in this additional way. The Special Prosecutor now seeks cert before judgment in the Court of Appeals.

DISCUSSION:

1. "Standing" of the Special Prosecutor as the Successful Party in the District Court to Petition for Cert before Judgment:

28 U.S.C. §1254 provides that "[c]ases in the courts of appeals may be reviewed by the Supreme Court. . . [b]y writ of certiorari granted upon the petition of any party to any civil or criminal case, before or after rendition of judgment. . . ." The Court has on at least three occasions affirmed its power under §1254 to issue a writ of certiorari before judgment on the petition of the successful

party in the District Court. Youngstown Sheet & Tube Co. v. Sawyer, 343 U.S. 579 (1952); United States v. United Mine Workers, 330 U.S. 258 (1947); United States v. Bankers' Trust, 294 U.S. 240 (1935). In the UMW case, the Court noted its authority under §1254's predecessor and briefly stated that prompt settlement of the case was in the public interest.

The prerequisites for review by writ of certiorari before judgment appear to be that the losing party note an appeal and that the record be docketed in the Court of Appeals. See Stern and Gressman, pp. 30 and 282. The suggestion that the record must be docketed in the Court of Appeals apparently stems from the §1254 authorization that "[c]ases in the courts of appeals may be reviewed by. . . ." See also Gay v. Buff, 292 U.S. 25, 30 (1934), where the Court stated that the sole essential of this Court's jurisdiction to review is that there be a case pending in the Court of Appeals.

It should be noted that the Youngstown, UMW and Bankers' Trust cases stand only for the proposition that an appeal by a party aggrieved in a case then pending in the Court of Appeals, may be "transferred" at the petition of the party successful in the District Court to the Court for hearing. It is doubtful whether in the absence of an appeal to the Court of Appeals by the losing party, the successful party has standing to petition for review.

2. Authority of the Special Prosecutor to Conduct and Argue His Case before the Court:

The authority and powers of the Special Prosecutor stem originally from Department of Justice Order No. 517-73, 38 FR 14688. That order was issued on May 31, 1973 by then AG Richardson under his authority to "make such provisions as he considers appropriate authorizing the performance by any other officer, employee, or agency of the Department of Justice of any function of the Attorney General." 28 U.S.C. §510. The order establishes, within the Department of Justice, a Special Prosecutor who, with respect to a very broad spectrum of "Watergate" matters, is delegated authority for, inter alia:

> Determining whether or not to contest the assertion of "Executive privilege" or any other testimonial privilege;
>
> . . . .

> Initiating and conducting prosecutions, framing indictments, filing informations, and handling all apsects of any cases within his jurisdiction. . . including any appeals.

The original order was subsequently abolished, 38 FR 29466, and then in substance reissued as Department of Justice Order No. 551-73 by then acting AG Bork on November 2. 38 FR 30738. [It appears that no relevant orders have been issued by AG Saxbe.]

That the AG has delegatable authority to conduct and argue cases before the Court seems clear. The SG is appointed to assist the AG in the performance of the latter's duties, 28 U.S.C. §505; all functions of other officers of the Department of Justice are vested in the AG, 28 U.S.C. §509; and "Except when the Attorney General in a particular case directs otherwise, the Attorney General and the Solicitor General shall conduct and argue suits and appeals in the Supreme Court. . . in which the United States is interested." 28 U.S.C. §518(a).

3. Procedural Posture of the Case, a Jurisdictional Question:

The Special Prosecutor states that the President has filed a timely notice of appeal and footnotes a cite to Nixon v. Sirica, supra at 707 n. 21, where the Court of Appeals held, in a footnote, that an order of the type in issue here is appealable.

In Nixon v. Sirica, the President sought review in the Court of Appeals by mandamus. It appears that neither the Special Prosecutor nor the President considered Judge Sirica's order in that case appealable. In fact, the President's counsel was of the opinion that an appeal of the order was barred by United States v. Ryan, 402 U.S. 530 (1971), where the Court held that an order denying a motion to quash a grand jury subpoena duces tecum was not final and therefore not appealable. See Reply Brief of Richard M. Nixon at 2, United States v. Sirica, 487 F.2d 700 (D.C. Cir. 1973). While the Special Prosecutor initially agreed that the order was not a final judgment appealable under 28 U.S.C. 1291 or an interlocutory order appealable pursuant to 28 U.S.C. §1292, he subsequently adopted the position of Judge Sirica that the order was appealable under 28 U.S.C. §1291 as well as contending that the order was appealable by the Government under 28 U.S.C. §1292(a)(1) or 18 U.S.C. §3731 and he filed a notice of appeal. See Answer of the Special Prosecutor at para. 2b; Answer of Respondent [Judge Sirica] to Petition for Writ of Mandamus, pp. 5-6; and Reply Memorandum for the United States at 5 n. 1, United States v. Sirica, supra. The Court of Appeals heard the case on the President's petition for writ of mandamus pursuant to its authority under the All Writs statute, 28 U.S.C. §1651, but, in footnote 21 made known its opinion that it also considered that it had appellate jurisdiction. In the footnote, the Court of Appeals reasoned that the final order doctrine, as a normal prerequisite to a federal appeal, is not a barrier where it operates to leave the suitor "powerless to avert the mischief of the order." Perlman v. United States, 247 U.S. 7, 13 (1918). But see United States v. Ryan, supra at 533-34 where the Court distinguished Perlman on the ground that Ryan, unlike Perlman, was free to refuse compliance with the grand jury subpoena and able to obtain full review of his claims before undertaking any burden of compliance with the subpoena.

The Special Prosecutor also states that the President has sought review of the District Court's order in the Court of Appeals on a petition for writ of mandamus. The particular posture of the case appears jurisdictionally significant. If the President's appeal is found to be proper, there would seem to be no bar to review under §1254. See Youngstown Sheet & Tube Co. v. Sawyer, supra, and other cases cited in section 1 of this discussion. If, on the other hand, appeal of the District Court's order is found not to lie, review under §1254 would then appear to have to be based on the mandamus action. While the Court has certiorari jurisdiction under §1254 to review the judgment of a Court of Appeals in a mandamus action, see Schlagenhauf v. Holder, 379, 379 U.S. 104 (1964), I can find no precedent for "transferring" a mandamus action pending in a Court of Appeals to this Court. It is possible, of course, that under the broad dicta of Gay v. Buff, supra, a mandamus action may be "a case pending in the circuit court of appeals" for purposes of the similarly broad language of §1254.

Another aspect of the mandamus side of this case is whether the Special Prosecutor is a "party" to the mandamus action for purposes of seeking review under §1254. Assumedly, the mandamus action is against Judge Sirica. In Sirica v. Nixon, supra, a mandamus action, the Special Prosecutor was apparently joined as a party respondent. The Special Prosecutor's "standing" in the present case is not stated in the pleadings. In this respect, it is noted that the Special Prosecutor has styled and framed his petition in a way that suggests he is seeking review of the President's appeal. It is not clear whether he is also seeking review of the mandamus action which was docketed as a separate case in the Court of Appeals. See petition p. 2 and n. 2.

4. Rule 20 Standard:

Under Rule 20, certiorari before judgment will be granted only upon "a showing that the case is of such imperative public importance as to justify the deviation from normal appellate processes and to require immediate settlement in this Court." The rule cites several examples of cases in which certiorari before judgment was granted. Although expedited review has been granted in several recent cases, it appears that the last case in which the Court granted a writ of certiorari before judgment was in Wilson v. Gerard, 354 U.S. 1 (1957). A brief review of the "imperative public importance" of these cases appears appropriate.

In Gerard, the Court granted the Government's Rule 20 petition to review an injunction issued by the District Court enjoining the Secretary of Defense from delivering an American soldier to Japanese authorities for trial on criminal charges in the Japanese courts. The Government contended that further delay in the matter would seriously aggravate an already unfortunate strain on United States-Japanese relations. In Youngstown Co. v. Sawyer, 343 U.S. 579 (1952), the issue of imperative public importance was the constitutional power of the President to take possession of and operate most of the Nation's steel mills. United States v. United Mine Workers, 330 U.S. 258 (1947), concerned the coal strike of 1947. In its opinion, the Court noted that prompt settlement of the case was in the public interest. 330 U.S. at 269. Ex parte Quirin, 317 U.S. 1 (1942), was the German Saboteurs case, in which the issues were considered so urgent that the Court convened in a special term during the summer to grant the petition and to hear argument. There are also the several depression era cases. Carter v. Carter Coal Co., 298 U.S. 238 (1936), involved the constitutionality of the Bituminus Coal Conservation Act of 1935. In its opinion, the Court briefly stated that "[b]ecause of the importance of the question and the advantage of a speedy and final determination thereof, the writs were granted." 298 U.S. at 285. Rickert Rice Mills v. Rontenot (and seven companion cases), 297 U.S. 110 (1936), concerned the right of the Government to collect processing taxes levied under the Agricultural Adjustment Act of 1933. The petitioners there asserted that by reason of the provisions of the Act it would be impossible to recover taxes collected, even though the act were unconstitutional, since the Act prohibited recovery except upon a showing of facts not susceptible of proof. In Railroad Retirement Board v. Alton R. Co., 295 U.S. 330 (1935), the Court granted certiorari before judgment to review the decree of the Supreme Court of the District of Columbia granting an injunction against the enforcement of the Railroad Retirement Act of 1934. Lastly, in United States v. Bankers' Trust Co., 294 U.S. 240 (1935), the Court granted certiorari before judgment to review two decisions sustaining the power of Congress to invalidate "gold clauses" in private money contracts. The total of all such gold clause obligations issued and outstanding was estimated at from 90 to 125 billion dollars.

In the present case, the Special Prosecutor refers to the importance of the constitutional issues involved, in their own right and in the context of the litigation in which they arise, and asserts that it is of imperative public importance that the issues be resolved as quickly as possible to permit the trial in the "Watergate cover-up case" to proceed as scheduled on September 9, 1974. The Special Prosecutor suggests that if certiorari is not granted, there would be a minimum delay of six months in the start of the trial. The Special Prosecutor also suggests that judicial efficiency will be served by granting certiorari in that the Court of Appeals previously has considered and ruled on the principal constitutional issues presented for review by this petition.

5. Questions of Fact:

The decision of the District Court in ordering the issuance of the subpoena here in issue was based on factual determinations in at least two respects. Under the "good cause" requirement of Rule 17(c), Judge Sirica found that (1) the subpoenaed materials are evidentiary and relevant; (2) they are not otherwise procurable reasonably in advance of trial; (3) the party cannot properly prepare for trial without them, and failure to obtain them may delay the trial; and (4) the application is made in good faith and does not constitute a "fishing expedition." Opinion and Order pp. 16-17. Judge Sirica also found that the Special Prosecutor's submissions constitute a prima facie showing adequate to rebut with respect to each of the subpoenaed material the presumption of the President's "presumptively valid" confidentiality privilege, and that the Special Prosecutor's submissions constitute a demonstration of need sufficiently compelling to warrant judicial examination in chambers incident to weighing claims of the privilege. The President contested these factual questions in the District and it may be presumed that he will preserve them on review.

While it would not appear necessary that the Court reach these factual issues on the asserted jurisdictional claims of "Executive privilege" and "intra-branch controversy," if those claims are resolved against the President it would then seem necessary to address the merits of the District Court's factual findings. On the other hand, I do not understand the President's claim to be that he is immune from process but, rather, that under the separation of powers doctrine his assertion of Executive privilege is final and not reviewable by this Branch. In this context, the Court may first wish to address the 17(c) issue regarding the propriety of the issuance of the subpoena. The question may be academic. In any event, I think it can be anticipated that the President's response will address the question of whether review should be granted in light of the factual issues involved.

The District Court did not reach the Brady issue posed by the defendants below. I am not sure what bearing, if any, this issue has on the present matter. I would note, however, the motion filed by defendant Strachan with respect to the subpoenaed material and also the case of United States v. Ehrlichman, et al. now pending before Judge Gesell in the District Court.

6. Nixon v. Sirica:

The Special Prosecutor contends that the en banc decision of the Court of Appeals controls the issue of Executive privilege raised by the President in this case. Although there appear to be important distinctions between the two cases, i.e., the subpoena in issue in Nixon v. Sirica was a grand jury subpoena and there were no defendants involved in that action, the opinion of the Court of Appeals seems broad enough to control the claim in this case. The President apparently conceded this in the District Court. Petition at 11. I am not so sure, however, that the President is foreclosed

Exhibit 5.2—*Continued*

- 9 -

from contesting the issue as suggested by the Special Prosecutor at p. 9 n. 7 of his petition. See Sunshine Anthracite Coal Co. v. Adkins, 310 U.S. 381, 402-404. The parties may not be "essentially the same." The grand jury would appear to be a substantially different party from the Special Prosecutor and the nature of the subpoenas involved would further tend to distinguish the two cases, at least for purposes of *res judicata*.

Jim Ginty
James B. Ginty

litigation at that time. By the conference's end, however, Powell, Douglas, Stewart, and Burger switched their votes. The final tally in conference was 6:2 to grant the expedited petition.[12]

As Brennan noted:

> initially, majority sentiment was not for bypass of the Court of Appeals. Two of the Justices were definitely against bypass and three others leaned that way. Only two of us felt strongly that the nation would think we had 'let the people down' if we didn't bypass.[13]

Brennan urged and pleaded with his peers to expedite because, "after two years of Watergate, it was time the nation had access to the evidence that would reveal the truth about Watergate."[14]

Justice Douglas, for one, "strongly opposed taking the case." He felt that the Court of Appeals "would quickly affirm the District Court, and we could quickly deny certiorari. We should deny it because the legislative and constitutional issues were frivolous and, as they involved impeachment, were political."[15] Brennan's notes indicated that Douglas wanted the case to remain at the Court of Appeals and that Douglas believed "it would be shocking to withhold exculpatory material that would free men." Although he "prefer[red] not to bypass," Douglas did say that he would "acquiesce if the Court grants."[16]

Blackmun, according to Brennan's notes, believed that "a six month delay in a criminal case is no irreparable injury. . . . It may be an unpopular decision but I'd deny."[17] Stewart also voiced some misgivings and thought that "a criminal trial can be put off without real damage." He did not see this litigation "qualifying" under Rule 20.[18] White, too, was reluctant to bypass the Court of Appeals because "Jaworski's application doesn't really demonstrate immediate need." According to Brennan, White then stated that the expedited appeal was "just a transparent attempt to have an impact on [the] impeachment proceeding. I don't think we should let ourselves be used that way." White clearly "prefer[red] to deny."[19]

So, too, did Justice Powell. On the merits of the case, he was "inclined to say [that Nixon] can't claim privilege to keep material from defense"; procedurally, however, Powell "would expedite any appeal from the Court of Appeals but not under Rule 20."[20]

According to the Brennan docket notes, Marshall briefly commented that he didn't "see why we should go to the Court of Appeals."[21] Chief Justice Burger, however, focussed essentially on the substantive issue of executive privilege.[22]

Brennan, however, "felt strongly that we should take the cases," Douglas wrote. Evidently, after a while, "so did Marshall." Furthermore, Douglas recalled Brennan stating that if the Court declined to hear the Nixon case, "he would write in dissent." As the discussion continued, there "developed an opinion in the minds of Stewart, . . . and Powell that the cases should be taken."[23]

Evidently the feeling grew among five of the justices—joined strategically at the end of the discussion by Burger—"that the Court had a 'duty' to step in and clarify the Watergate mess."[24] Brennan saw the case as one that, "in the context of the times, called for the kind of opinion we had in 1958 with *Cooper v. Aaron*."[25] His views, clearly enunciated, brought Brennan's hesitant colleagues to the view that it was the Court's "duty to our institution and to the public not to delay" hearing the case.[26]

The final vote in the May 31 conference was 6:2 (see exhibit 5.3); Blackmun and White continued to believe that Rule 20 should not be employed to grant certiorari. Brennan's arguments, however, convinced Powell, Stewart, Marshall, and Douglas. Burger joined the majority in order to be able to write the opinion of the Court in *U.S. v. Nixon*.

Later that day the Supreme Court's Journal noted (without acknowledging the split vote) that the petition for writ of certiorari to the Court of Appeals and motion for an expedited schedule was "granted."[27] The Order established dates for the filing of briefs (by July 1) and oral argument (by July 8), and noted that Rehnquist did not participate in the proceedings.[28] (See exhibit 5.4.)

THE COURT'S AGENDA AFTER GRANTING THE PETITION TO EXPEDITE

Clearly, the justices were persuaded by Brennan's lengthy arguments that the Court had the responsibility to "resolve the

Exhibit 5.3
The Final Vote in the May 31 Conference Session

Court	*Voted on*.................., *19*...	
Argued ...., *19*...	*Assigned* ...., *19*...	No. 73-1766
Submitted ...., *19*...	*Announced* ...., *19*...	

UNITED STATES OF AMERICA

vs.

RICHARD M. NIXON, PRESIDENT OF THE U.S. et al.

From 6-2, votes changed LP + PS on ground every other institutions has [illegible] & we have duty to see institutions and to public seem to be one of these – so set for July 8

	HOLD FOR	CERT.		JURISDICTIONAL STATEMENT				MERITS		MOTION		AB-SENT	NOT VOT-ING
		G	D	N	POST	DIS	AFF	REV	AFF	G	D		
Rehnquist, J.		out											
Powell, J.		✓											
Blackmun, J.			✓										
Marshall, J.		✓											
White, J.			✓										
Stewart, J.		✓											
Brennan, J.		✓											
Douglas, J.		✓											
Burger, Ch. J.		✓											

Exhibit 5.4
Supreme Court *Journal*: Petition for Writ of Certiorari in *U.S. v. Nixon* (1974)

(JOUNRAL) FRIDAY, MAY 31, 1974 591

SUPREME COURT OF THE UNITED STATES

Present: Mr. Chief Justice Burger, Mr. Justice Douglas, Mr. Justice Brennan, Mr. Justice Stewart. Mr. Justice White, Mr. Justice Marshall, Mr. Justice Blackmun, Mr. Justice Powell, and Mr. Justice Rehnquist.

CERTIORARI GRANTED

No. 73–1766. United States, petitioner, v. Richard M. Nixon. President of the United States, et al. Petition for writ of certiorari to the United States Court of Appeals for the District of Columbia Circuit and motion for an expedited schedule granted. The parties shall exchange and file briefs by 1:00 p.m. on June 21 and any responsive brief shall be filed by July 1, 1974. Oral argument is set for July 8, 1974, at 10:00 a.m. Each party is allowed one hour for argument. Mr. Justice Rehnquist took no part in the consideration or decision of this motion and petition.

×

political agony which the country was undergoing."[29] Immediately after the May 31, 1974 decision, the brethren then had to confront the fluidity of judicial choice in a case involving the very essence of presidential power. Contrary to contemporary accounts of the Supreme Court's internal activities surrounding *Nixon*,[30] it was not an easily resolved nor an easily written opinion.

NOTES

1. Congressional Quarterly, *Watergate: Chronology of a Crisis* (Washington, D.C.: Congressional Quarterly Press, 1975), p. 619.
2. Robert Woodward and Scott Armstrong, *The Brethren: Inside the Supreme Court* (New York: Simon and Schuster, 1979), p. 290.
3. Leon Jaworski, *The Power and the Right: The Prosecution of Watergate* (New York: Reader's Digest Press, 1976), p. 148.

4. *Youngstown Sheet and Tube Co. v. Sawyer* 343 *U.S.* 579 (1952).

5. Jaworski, *The Power and the Right*, pp. 150, ff.

6. Phillip Lacovara interview, November 21, 1987, Hofstra University, Hempstead, New York. Asked by a *Time* reporter whether he planned to resist or contest a 6:2 or 5:3 Supreme Court ruling, Nixon responded: "No, I had that as a possible option, but I hadn't planned it in advance, saying if we get one or two votes, that then we will resist it. No." Nixon interview, *Time*, April 2, 1990, p. 46.

7. Ibid.

8. Ibid.

9. During the recent Iran-Contra litigation, the White House and the Justice Department prepared court documents that argued that President Ronald Reagan and Vice President George Bush did not have to honor a subpoena issued to force them to testify in Court about the Iran-Contra Affair. "It's not a question of the merits of this case one way or the other," one official said. "Forcing them to testify at the trial would be a hazardous inroad into the powers and prerogatives of the executive branch." The prime argument the Justice Department was to make was based on executive privilege: "Presidents just don't testify in Court." As Laurence Tribe noted, executive privilege protects the office, not the man. Philip Shenon, "Reagan and Bush to Fight North Trial Subpoenas," *The New York Times*, January 1, 1989.

10. MTTC, May 25, 1974, Brennan Papers, Box 329, LC, Washington, D.C.

11. Letter, Rehnquist to Burger, Brennan Papers, Box 329, LC, Washington, D.C.

12. See Figure A.

13. Letter, Brennan to Ball, January 4, 1988.

14. Ibid. He also wrote that, "since most of the Court's cases for the Term had already been decided, the Court was in the rare position of being able to give its undivided attention to this single case."

15. William O. Douglas, *The Court Years* (New York: Random House, 1980), pp. 139–40. Brennan, too, believed that Nixon's substantive argument was without merit. "Based on some exhaustive research, I had concluded that the President's claim of absolute executive privilege was plainly without constitutional foundation, and that we should say so at the earliest opportunity, lest the nation lose all confidence in the criminal justice system." Letter, Brennan to Ball, January 8, 1988.

16. Docket Book, 1973 Term, Brennan Papers, Box 423, LC.

17. Ibid.

18. Ibid.

19. Ibid.

20. Ibid.
21. Ibid.
22. Ibid.
23. Douglas, *Court Years*, pp. 139–40.
24. Ibid.
25. William J. Brennan quoted in Jeffrey T. Leeds, "A Life on the Court," *New York Times Sunday Magazine*, Oct. 5, 1986, p. 25.
26. Docket Book, 1973 Term, Brennan Papers, Box 423, LC.
27. *Supreme Court Journal*, May 31, 1974, p. 591.
28. Ibid.
29. Paul J. Mishkin, "Great Cases and Soft Law: A Comment on U.S. v. Nixon," *UCLA Law Review*, 22 (1974): 90.
30. See, for example, Nina Totenberg, "Behind the Marble, Beneath the Robes," *New York Times Sunday Magazine*, March 16, 1975. She claimed that Justice Potter Stewart "argued forcefully that it was up to the judiciary to settle quickly on an issue that was so terribly paralyzing the other institutions of government and so deeply affecting the national well being." Further, she wrote that Stewart and Douglas had to persuade Brennan and Marshall (!) to vote in favor of granting the expedited granting of the writ of certiorari (p. 58).

6

U.S. v. Nixon, II: Written Briefs and Oral Arguments

Once the writ of certiorari was granted, the lawyers for the parties to the dispute began to prepare their briefs for presentation to the Court. The justices, too, began to review seriously these threshold and substantive issues and, with their law clerks, they began to develop tentative answers to these constitutional issues.

The justices of the Supreme Court, together as a full court only since the appointment and confirmation of Powell and Rehnquist in 1972, had in less than one month (May 31 to June 15) granted certiorari in an expedited fashion, raised fundamental threshold constitutional questions about the separation of powers, and drawn together in an institutional duty to resolve "the Watergate mess." The next stage, prior to the oral argument scheduled for July 8, required the justices to review the briefs and to prepare their responses to the legal and political questions raised in the case of *U.S. v. Nixon*.

THE UNINDICTED CO-CONSPIRATOR (RICHARD M. NIXON) ISSUE BEFORE THE COURT

Furthermore, a flurry of additional appeals in early June led to a discussion about whether the Court should respond to the legal issue associated with the Grand Jury's naming of President Nixon as an unindicted co-conspirator in the Watergate coverup activities.[1] On June 3, Phillip Lacovara, counsel to the Watergate special prosecutor, wrote to the clerk of the Court "requesting instruction on how to proceed with two aspects of this case":[2]

1. Printing of materials from the sealed files, and
2. Briefing and arguing a legal issue that "turns inextricably upon information currently under seal."[3]

Evidently, according to the counsel for the special prosecutor, the sealed materials contained information that "in our judgment is necessary to the Court's informed decision on the executive privilege question." Under Sirica's May 13 order, however, their office was "not permitted to disclose this information to anyone."[4]

On June 4, in response to the Lacovara letter, the justices were instructed by Burger that the "sealed" materials were in the Court vault and were "available to any Justice. We should be prepared to resolve those questions," Burger wrote, "at the Friday conference."[5] (Prior to that Conference, the *Washington Post* and the *Washington Star* had leaked portions of the sealed materials that had been delivered to the House Committee on Impeachment. The leaked data indicated that Nixon had been named by the Grand Jury as an unindicted co-conspirator.) On June 10 Jaworski and St. Clair submitted a joint motion requesting the Court to unseal the record. The next day, however, six defendants wrote a memo "respectfully objecting to the release of the sealed materials to anyone except the defendants' counsel."[6]

The June 14 Conference adopted the Stewart response to the new appeals: the Court denied the motion to unseal except for an extract that had already been leaked.[7] The Court thus made public the following extract from the Grand Jury's sealed record. In so doing, as the president's counsel pointed out in his written brief an in oral argument before the justices, the Court provided additional data for the public and the congressional investigators to consume.

> . . . The grand jury, by a vote of 19-0, determined that there is probable cause to believe that Richard M. Nixon (among others) was a member of a conspiracy to defraud the United States and to obstruct justice charged in Count 1 of the instant indictment, and the Grand Jury authorized the Special Prosecutor to identify Richard M. Nixon (among others) as an unindicted co-conspirator in connection with subsequent legal proceedings in this case.[8]

Nixon's lawyers then petitioned the Court to decide whether the Grand Jury had the right "under the Constitution" to so charge a sitting president as an unindicted co-conspirator. While Justice Douglas's early July draft to the Conference argued that the issue was a "political question" because the Court was being brought into the ongoing impeachment proceedings,[9] the Court majority sidestepped the issue entirely.[10]

THE JUSTICES PONDER THE LEGAL AND POLITICAL ISSUES, JUNE 1974

While Justice Rehnquist was busily engaged in arranging VIP seating for the oral argument session that was set for July 8,[11] the others were engaged in the difficult, often painful, task of reviewing the submitted briefs and developing their tentative responses to the key issues of jurisdiction, justiciability, and executive privilege. The fluidity of judicial choice was well under way. It began with their review of the lengthy written briefs from the parties to the dispute: Leon Jaworski for the special prosecutor and James St. Clair of the president. (See exhibit 6.1.)

THE SPECIAL PROSECUTOR'S MAIN BRIEF IN *NIXON*

The special prosecutor's brief, submitted to Jaworski and Lacovara to the justices in early June 1974, examined what were

Exhibit 6.1
Memorandum from Michael Rodak, Jr., to Chief Justice Burger

SUPREME COURT OF THE UNITED STATES
OFFICE OF THE CLERK
WASHINGTON, D. C. 20543

June 7, 1974

MEMORANDUM TO THE CHIEF JUSTICE

Confirming our recent conversation, the Special Appearance and Motion to Lift Protective Order filed by Mr. St. Clair was filed in view of the headlines that appeared in yesterday's Washington Post and Evening Star Newspapers. The cross petition for writ of certiorari was to preserve the question which they were not sure would have been encompassed or included in the questions raised by the petition filed in No. 73-1766 and was taken as a precautionary measure. The motion for leave to file the cross petition under seal was a further precautionary measure to insure that they did not violate the original protective order issued by Judge Sirica.

I have been informed by Mr. Lacovara that the hearing this afternoon before Judge Sirica was a very brief hearing wherein he promptly advised counsel that he was vacating his protective order. He further informed counsel that he has no jurisdiction of the record and of the case, and whether the record was to remain sealed was a matter for the Supreme Court to decide. He, in effect, said that if the records were still in his custody he would remove any seal on them. Mr. Lacovara has further advised me that his order is being reduced to writing and we hopefully may get a copy late this afternoon.

Respectfully submitted,

Michael Rodak, Jr.

Michael Rodak, Jr.
Clerk

P.S.: A copy of Judge Sirica's order was just received and is attached hereto.

MRjr.

for the prosecutors some very important questions. What were the powers of a Grand Jury with respect to the president's being cited by the Grand Jury as an unindicted co-conspirator? Did the federal judiciary have authority to hear the case and issue orders to the president? Was the president subject to a judicial order directing compliance with a subpoena *duces tecum*? What was the scope of the presidential claim of executive privilege?

For Jaworski and Lacovara, the Court was confronted with a "live, concrete justiciable controversy" that had to be resolved by the brethren.[12] They forcefully argued that the litigation was not an intrabranch dispute outside the purview of the federal courts. The "fundamental point" they made, at the very beginning of their brief, was that the president "is decidedly *not* the sovereign."[13] In *Nixon*, given the responsibility of the attorney general and appointees of the attorney general such as the special prosecutor to conduct civil and criminal affairs in court, the president must be seen as a third party.

Therefore, they argued, it is "clear beyond peradventure" that the special prosecutor has "standing" to seek enforcement of the subpoena against the president. Jaworski has "such a personal stake in the outcome of the controversy as to assure that concrete adverseness."[14] For Nixon to frame the controversy as "a mere 'intraexecutive branch' dispute, as counsel for the President did, seems to invoke [a] sterile conceptualism [that was] long ago discarded."[15] If the justices "look beyond the President's formalistic objections to the Court's jurisdiction," they will note jurisdiction and resolve the dispute between the president and the special prosecutor.[16] The federal courts, they insisted, using their Article III jurisdiction to hear all cases arising under the Constitution, have both the duty and the power to resolve the controversy.

Regarding Nixon's claim of an absolute executive privilege, Jaworski maintained that all federal courts "have rejected a claim of absolute executive privilege to withhold evidence merely upon the assertion of the executive that disclosure would not be in the public interest."[17] While acknowledging "legitimate interests in secrecy," the brief urged the Court to define and apply a qualified privilege in the instant case.

While separation of powers is an important constitutional

theme, that doctrine, they argued, "does not give the executive any constitutional immunity from judicial orders for the production of evidence."[18] The general public, they argued, has the right to every man's evidence, including the president. The history of the constitutional period, the brief concluded, is "persuasive against the claim of an absolute Presidential prerogative to be immune from the judicial process."[19]

Getting to the heart of the practical dilemma, Jaworski noted that the issue of executive privilege in *Nixon* was not associated with the typical communications within the executive branch that, in the past, have remained confidential.[20] Rather, in *Nixon*, there was a "*prima facie* showing that the officials participating in the deliberations did so as part of a continuing criminal plan. . . . [Therefore] the President is foreclosed from invoking a privilege that exists only to protect and promote the legitimate conduct of the Nation's affairs."[21] Discussions in the White House that are in furtherance of a "criminal conspiracy cannot be subsumed within executive privilege."[22]

After arguing that the subpoena was issued in accordance with Rule 17c of the Federal Rules of Criminal Procedure, the special prosecutor's main brief ended with the plea that Sirica's order directing the president to comply with the subpoena should be affirmed by the Court.

THE PRESIDENT'S MAIN BRIEF IN *NIXON*

James D. St. Clair, the president's chief counsel in the Watergate litigation, took the predicted absolutist tack with regard to the absolute immunity of the president to employ (or not) executive privilege. Further, the brief strenuously argued that because of the separation of powers doctrine, the federal courts, including the U.S. Supreme Court, lacked jurisdiction to hear what was essentially an intrabranch dispute. Even if there was the authority to hear *Nixon*, the "political question" doctrine made the case a nonjusticiable one.[23] There was also no showing by Jaworski of the compelling need for the tapes in the criminal case he was preparing for the Fall 1974.

St. Clair urged the Court to reflect on the "extraordinary"

impact of judicial involvement in the Watergate matter at a time when the Congress was beginning its impeachment inquiry. "It is, in effect, an extraordinary proceeding intrinsically related to the move now pending in the Congress to impeach the president of the United States."[24]

For the president, the case, "at its core,"[25] was a classic separation of powers one and all other considerations were secondary. For Nixon's lawyers, "preserving the integrity of separation of powers is vital to the preservation of our Constitution as a living body of fundamental law."[26] Under this doctrine, according to the president, the "Judiciary is without jurisdiction to intervene in the intra-branch dispute between the President and the Special Prosecutor."[27]

The president, it was argued, has ultimate authority over all decisions involving executive branch subordinates. Nixon, not having delegated that power to any other body, retains final and full authority to act or not as he so determines. While not questioning the Court's use of judicial review in other areas,[28] based on the separation of powers concept, the brief challenged the "authority of the Court or any branch of government to intervene in a solely intra-branch dispute, even at the request of a disputant."[29] Clearly, for the president and counsel, the matter was not within the jurisdiction of the Court for that reason and because it was a nonjusticiable "political question."

Finally, St. Clair maintained that "inherent in the executive power vested in the president under Article II of the Constitution is executive privilege, generally recognized as a derivative of the separation of powers doctrine."[30] As such, it is categorically nonreviewable by the Court. Thus, at every legal/jurisprudential juncture, the president's counsel argued that the president and only the president could make the critical decisions.

With the briefs now digested, the brethren were ready to grapple with the hard issues. Concerned about and aware of the time factor, the justices were eager to share their thoughts with each other, and so the process of circulating drafts and developing a consensus began after the June 14 Conference

Session ended. In that Conference they had agreed that "exchanges of memoranda would be welcomed."[31]

THE FLUIDITY OF CHOICE IN THE *NIXON* LITIGATION

On July 5, Justice Douglas circulated the first of his eight draft opinions written in the *Nixon* case. It was a thirty-page note that focused on the major issues, both procedural and substantive. "I enclose herewith an explanatory memorandum in the Nixon cases which I prepared to expedite my own resolution of the main issues," he wrote.[32]

The Douglas opinion focused on four issues:

1. Appealability. Douglas believed the case could be appealed.
2. Justiciability. Jaworski did have standing because he was, ultimately, an appointee with authority derived directly from Congress. Douglas believed that Archibald Cox, Jaworski's predecessor, had been fired illegally by Acting Attorney General Robert Bork because that office "was established explicitly to be an independent agency in response to the public demand for a prosecutor who was not subject to the direction of the President whose activities were intertwined with the investigation which need to conducted."[33]
3. Executive privilege. There is "no executive privilege of the President which justifies withholding these materials from the District Court." It was, Douglas decided, not appropriate for Nixon to use a concept that enables him, not the federal courts, "to pass on the materiality or relevance of the withheld material in the trial of the defendants." ". . . To allow [Nixon] to conceal from a court information which may be critical to the fairness of a trial of named defendants would be a monstrous affront to the rule of law under which we live."[34] (In his eighth version of his opinion, circulated on July 20, Douglas wrote that it was a "travesty to think of this case in terms of the so-called executive privilege. Every citizen, high or low, has a right to privacy and confidentiality concerning his conversations except as they be reached by process for use in a civil or criminal trial. This present controversy is a prelude to a serious criminal trial. In that setting it stands on no higher footing than does a subpoena issued against a member of the Mafia."[35])
4. Unindicted co-conspirator. For Douglas, as was pointed out earlier,

it was a nonjusticiable issue. "Beyond question," he wrote, "that issue is a 'political' issue. . . ."[36]

The strongly worded memo from Douglas was followed, on July 6, by a draft opinion written by Powell that "reflected [his] thinking after rather intensive study for the past two weeks."[37] In contrast to Douglas's urging a rejection of the executive privilege argument, Powell's draft was very deferential to the president on that issue. After briefly outlining reasons why he believed the Court had jurisdiction and that there was a justiciable case, he turned to executive privilege and "standards and procedures governing the exercise of judicial authority to order the president to comply with a subpoena."[38]

In his draft, Powell spoke of the "ultimate authority to decide whether, in a particular case, confidentiality must give way to some greater public interest [and that the judgment] resides in that branch whose constitutional responsibilities are more gravely affected." Powell, to the dismay of some of his brethren, was providing a basis for the president's continuing refusal to provide the tapes to the special prosecutor.

Powell labelled his "views and conclusions stated [as] tentative and subject, of course, to oral argument and our discussion at conference."[39] While he said that defining the "precise contours of the separation of powers concept is a task for the Courts," for Powell, however, the President had the "*ultimate authority* to decide whether in a particular case confidentiality must give way" (emphasis added). Furthermore, he wrote, the Supreme Court has to accept the constitutional principle, because "the interest in confidentiality pertains to the President's effective exercise of his executive powers, [that] it is nevertheless constitutionally based." In this light, Powell wrote, regarding the validity of the issuance of the subpoena under Rule 17c, that "absent compelling justification, competing societal interests, the courts cannot presume to order the President to produce confidential materials."[40] As if to temporize his blatant support of the president's position, Powell then stated that

nothing in the concept of separation of powers . . . compels the conclusion that . . . the decision whether to sacrifice confidentiality in a particular case in singularly committed exclusively to [Nixon's] discretion and cannot be reviewed or overridden by the judicial branch.[41]

Following this was his discussion of the procedures and standards for judicial determination of whether, once the president invokes privilege, there was "compelling justification" in the case. Powell, much to the chagrin of Douglas, Brennan, and Marshall, wrote that the "Court must require a special showing from the moving party [Jaworski if the president invokes the privilege]." If the president argued that the release of the subpoenaed materials "would prove injurious to the public interest, he may invoke executive privilege." At this point, a court "must require a special showing from the moving party." Jaworski had to show the necessity of the subpoenaed materials "to the ends of justice."[42] If the showing was made, then an order must issue for the president to produce the subpoenaed materials.

Clearly, ominously, the Powell draft was much, much closer to the Nixon position—certainly closer than Douglas's acid view. It was received by some of his brethren with deep concern. They busily concluded their drafts in order to quickly respond to Powell's adoration of the presidency.

A few days later, July 8, the morning of the oral argument, Justices Brennan and Stewart circulated their memos on the case. Brennan's was the shorter of the two and was in direct response to Powell's circulation.

> Although greatly impressed by Lewis' analysis in his memorandum . . . , I think his [executive privilege] Part IV requires some expansion and I am taking the liberty of circulating the attached in the hope that it may serve to focus that problem in our conference discussion.[43]

Brennan argued that Rule 17c was adequate to protect the president "from unnecessary interference or harassment." In cases involving the president, "appellate review, in deference to the comity properly accorded a coordinate branch of government, should be particularly meticulous to insure that the standards of Rule 17c have been correctly applied." Brennan's position: Nixon should "transmit directly to the District Court those materials for which no specific claim of privilege limited to national defense, foreign relations or domestic security is made."[44]

Stewart's memo was a more reflective essay addressing the question of court jurisdiction and justiciability. He rejected St. Clair's suggestions that it was an internal dispute and a nonjusticiable political issue. For Stewart, Jaworski was an employee appointed under congressional guidelines and could not be dismissed by Nixon.[45]

THE ORAL ARGUMENT BEFORE THE COURT

The case was argued before the justices on Monday, July 8, 1974. Jaworski spoke first and immediately raised the basic constitutional question when he asked who was the arbiter of the Constitution. St. Clair's arguments before the Court contained a categorical defense of absolute presidential immunity from every kind of criminal investigation unless the president decided that "in the public interest" the requested data could be turned over to a prosecutor.

An active eight-person Supreme Court interrupted the lawyers continually: Jaworski recalled that he was interrupted 115 times during his presentation. Justice Douglas, for example, asked Jaworski if it was right that "we start with a Constitution that does not contain the words 'executive privilege.' " (To which Jaworski responded, "That is right, sir.")[46] For the special prosecutor, the heart of the matter was the issue of separation of powers:

> Now enmeshed in almost 500 pages of briefs, when boiled down, this case really presents one fundamental issue. Who is to be the arbiter of what the Constitution says? . . . In refusing to produce the evidence sought by a subpoena . . . in the criminal trial of the seven defendants—among them former chief aides and devotees—the President invokes the provisions of the Constitution. . . . In his public statements, as we all know, the President has embraced the Constitution as offering him support for his refusal to supply the subpoenaed tapes. Now the President may be right in how he reads the Constitution, but he may also be wrong. And if he is wrong, who is there to tell him so? And if there is no one, then the President, of course,

is free to pursue his course of erroneous interpretations. What then becomes of our constitutional form of government?[47]

This was a major question, one that went to the very "heart of our basic constitutional system,"[48] a question that the justices returned to time and again over the course of the *Nixon* decision process.

St. Clair began his oral presentation by pointing out that Jaworski had "not once" mentioned what was really involved in this case. "That is the co-pendency of impeachment proceedings before the House of Representatives, and the realistic fusion that has taken place with these two proceedings and the promise of continued fusing." He was interrupted by a justice who asked: "Well, these are none of our problems, are they?" St. Clair's answer: "I think, sir, they really are."[49]

He was also asked many questions—more than 200 in the course of the first hour of argument. Given his starting point that the president is the absolute, final determiner of the use of executive privilege and that the federal judiciary could not interpose without violating the separation of powers, these interruptions were not surprising. His view that the president was not subject to the processes of the law "unless he so determines he would give evidence"[50] was at odds with some of the justices' views. For St. Clair, the matter was outside the jurisdiction of the federal courts and a nonjusticiable intra-branch dispute to boot.

With oral arguments concluded, it was now time for the brethren to get down to the hard work of writing and editing the opinion of the Court in *Nixon*. It was to be a painful process.

NOTES

1. Assistant Attorney General Henry E. Petersen, on April 17, 1973, told President Nixon that a person labeled an unindicted co-conspirator "means that for one reason or another we don't want to charge them at the time. . . . You are just as guilty [as a person who was indicted]." Quoted in Congressional Quarterly *Watergate: Chronology of a Crisis* (Washington, D.C.: Congressional Quarterly Press, 1975), p. 653.

2. Phillip A. Lacovara to Michael Rodak, June 3, 1974, Douglas Papers, Box 1659, (Library of Congress), Washington, D.C.

3. Ibid.

4. Memo to the Conference (MTTC), June 4, 1974, Brennan Papers, Box 329, LC, Washington, D.C.

5. Ibid.

6. Defense Attorneys to Michael Rodak, June 11, 1974, Douglas Papers, Box 1659, LC, Washington, D.C.

7. MTTC, June 14, 1974, Brennan Papers, Box 329, LC, Washington, D.C.

8. 417 *U.S.* 960 (1974).

9. Douglas argued that the Court was asked to decide whether that judgment "is not competent evidence in impeachment proceedings. . . . [This was a "political question"] because all matters pertaining to the process of impeachment are beyond the reach of the judicial power. They rest exclusively in the political branch." William O. Douglas, MTTC, July 5, 1974, Box 1659, LC, Washington, D.C.

10. See Attachment B. The Douglas "disposition of the issue could only have given comfort to the White House. By not confirming the Grand Jury's authority, it might enable the President to discredit both its action and that of the Special Prosecutor who had relied on its work." Schwartz, *Unpublished Opinions of the Burger Court* (New York: Oxford University Press, 1987), p. 156.

11. See his MTTC, June 11 and June 24, 1974, Box 1659, WODP LC, Washington, D.C.

12. Brief for the United States, *U.S. v. Richard M. Nixon,* On Writs of Certiorari to the U.S. Court of Appeals for the District of Columbia, June 1974, reprinted in Alan Westin and Leon Friedman, eds., *United States v. Nixon* (New York: Chelsea House, 1975), p. 224.

13. Ibid., p. 226.

14. Ibid., pp. 234-235.

15. Ibid., p. 235.

16. Ibid., p. 236.

17. Ibid., p. 243.

18. Ibid., p. 248.

19. Ibid., p. 258.

20. ". . . advisory opinion, recommendations and deliberations comprising a part of the process by which governmental decisions and policies are formulated." Ibid., p. 266.

21. Ibid.

22. Ibid., p. 268. There has to be "an underlying public purpose" behind the use of the privilege.

23. See his Brief for the Respondent, Cross Petitioner, Richard M. Nixon, President of the United States, in *U.S. v. Nixon*, reprinted in Westin and Friedman, *U.S. v. Nixon*.

24. Ibid., p. 328. St. Clair argued, correctly, that the "court process is being used as a discovery tool for the impeachment proceedings—proceedings which the Constitution assigns to the Congress, not the courts. . . . Thus the effect, whatever the intent, of the discovery procedures being pressed by the Special Prosecutor would be to produce evidence for the Congress that the Congress could not obtain by its own procedures."

25. Ibid., p. 327.

26. Ibid.

27. Ibid., p. 329. Furthermore, the brief stated, the intra-branch dispute "raises a political question which the federal courts lack jurisdiction to decide." Ibid., at 330.

28. Nixon claimed there was no dispute regarding judicial review of conflicts between co-equal branches nor did the brief dispute the power of the Court to "negate an act performed by one branch in excess of its constitutionally delegated authority." Ibid., p. 338.

29. Ibid.

30. Ibid., p. 330.

31. MTTC, July 6, 1974, Brennan Papers, Box 329, LC, Washington, D.C.

32. MTTC, July 5, 1974, Douglas Papers, Box 1659, LC, Washington, D.C.

33. Ibid.

34. Ibid.

35. MTTC, July 20, 1974, Douglas Papers, Box 1659, LC, Washington, D.C.

36. MTTC, July 5, 1974, Douglas Papers, Box 1659, LC, Washington, D.C.

37. MTTC, July 6, 1974, WODP LC, Box 1659, Washington, D.C.

38. MTTC, July 6, 1974, Brennan Papers, Box 329, LC, Washington, D.C.

39. Ibid.

40. Ibid.

41. Ibid.

42. Ibid.

43. MTTC, July 8, 1974, Brennan Papers, Box 329, LC.

44. Ibid.

45. MTTC, July 8, 1974, Douglas Papers, Box 1659, LC.

46. Westin and Friedman, *U.S. v. Nixon*, p. 530. At another point,

another justice asked Jaworski if he believed that executive privilege was a common law privilege. Jaworski again replied: "Yes, sir," (at 540).

47. Oral Argument in Friedman, *Nixon*, pp. 528–29.
48. Ibid., p. 529.
49. Ibid., p. 545.
50. Ibid., p. 549.

7

U.S. v. Nixon, III: The Substantive Debate among the Brethren

At the conclusion of the oral argument, the justices of the Court entered the critical group phase, the Conference Session, that was followed by the equally important opinion-creation time. Faced with some severe time constraints (the impending impeachment action in the House of Representatives), the brethren had to gear up for some serious consultations. They also needed to act quickly because the chief justice would probably want to write the opinion for the Court.

THE CRITICAL JULY 9, 1974, CONFERENCE SESSION

In the July 9 Conference Session, convened a day after the oral arguments, the justices unanimously agreed that there was jurisdiction to hear the case and that it was a justiciable controversy. There was some agreement about the Rule 17c application, although Justice Powell wrote that "we were not entirely in agreement as to the standard to be met in overcoming the privilege."[1] There was agreement that executive privilege did not bar the courts, under certain conditions, from ordering the president to turn over the requested tapes for an *in camera* court inspection.

The brethren, all of them, were of the belief that there was some type of limited, common law, executive privilege. As Powell wrote, in a July 12, 1974 "Dear Chief" letter, copied to all the brethren, they "were all in accord that there is a privilege of confidentiality with respect to presidential conversations and papers. We also agreed that it is a qualified privilege and not absolute or unreviewable; and, in this case, that the special prosecutor has made a showing which overcomes the privilege and justifies *in camera* review."[2]

On the unindicted co-conspirator issue, the justices voted without dissent to dismiss the petition as improvidently granted.[3] There was "no political question in either impending impeachment or otherwise. No reason to stay our hand," Brennan wrote. He noted that Justice Douglas proposed that the Court dismiss the issue because it was not relevant to the issue of discovery, and it was, insofar as it was relevant to Watergate, a political question.[4]

Furthermore, from Brennan's notes it is clear that all the brethren discussed the case openly. Burger viewed the case as falling within the Court's jurisdiction, as a "justiciable" case or controversy. He also believed that Rule 17c was appropriate and distinguished executive privilege from presidential privilege. Presidential privilege, Burger said, "was [a] qualified privilege limited to official duties." Who decides, he asked, "when it is no longer crucial?" Burger also noted that "conduct outside Article II [executive power] is not covered [under] presidential privilege."[5]

The Conference ended with strong consensus on all the legal issues raised on the briefs and oral arguments by counsel for the special prosecutor's office. In addition, the four justices—Douglas, Powell, Brennan, and Stewart—who had circulated memos prior to the Conference Session had greatly aided in the framing and answering of the legal questions: appealable, yes (8:0); justiciable, yes (8:0); Rule 17c appropriate as applied, yes (8:0); executive privilege not applicable in this case, yes (8:0).

Brennan wanted the Court to have the final opinion, if possible, formally signed by all the justices as was done by the Court in *Cooper v. Aaron* (1958).[6] Although he "went around to see everyone and tried to sell the idea . . . , it was a complete failure. Nobody agreed, not one."[7] Burger responded acidly in a Conference to that suggestion: "The responsibility [for writing the opinion] is on my shoulders."

According to tradition, Chief Justice Burger took the opinion. It was now his responsibility to write a most historic opinion that involved a major concept of the American constitutional system: the separation of powers. However, as was already happening prior to the oral argument and the July 9, 1974 Conference Session, the case took on the "characteriz[ation of an] 'opinion by committee.' "[8]

After the Conference ended, Justice Brennan visited his dear old friend colleague on the Court, the deathly ill former Chief Justice Earl Warren. Warren was in the Georgetown University Hospital. When Brennan told the "Super Chief" the news of the day, Warren murmured, "Thank God, thank God, thank God! If you don't do it this way, Bill, it's the end of the country as we have known it."[9] Warren had very little respect for the president. He had just recently written of Nixon that he was "the most despicable President this nation ever had. He was a cheat, a crook, and a liar, and he brought my country, which I love, into disrepute. Even worse than abusing his office, he abused the American people."[10] A few hours later, Earl Warren died and, in a twist of irony caught by the brethren and others, his old nemesis, Richard Nixon, participated in the eulogies for the "Super Chief."

THE SUPREME COURT SEEKS AGREEMENT ON THE RATIONALE FOR ITS VOTE IN *U.S. V. NIXON*, JULY 1974

Although the chief justice took on the awesome task of writing the opinion for the Court, and although the justices had rejected Brennan's *Cooper* suggestions, the reality, the outline seen even before the July 9 Conference Session, was an opinion by an eight-person group. An undated "opinion outline" in the Brennan file indicates that seven of the eight had a hand

Exhibit 7.1
Undated Opinion Outline, *U.S. v. Nixon* (1974)—Justice Brennan's File

Opinion Outline

I. Facts [HAB]

II. Appealability [WOD]

III. Intra-branch dispute [WJB or beefed-up WEB version]

IV. Rule 17(c) [BRW]

V. [Merits of executive privilege: WEB; LFP as revised by PS]

VI. Standards to be met before in camera inspection is ordered [LFP as revised by WJB]

VII. The Court's judgment and order [WJB]

in the crafting of the opinion. (See exhibit 7.1.) According to the Brennan note, the breakdown went as follows: Blackmun, facts; Douglas, appealability; Brennan/Burger, justiciability; White, Rule 17c; Burger/Powell with Stewart revisions, executive privilege; Powell and Brennan revisions, Standards met before *In Camera* inspection; Brennan, Court's judgment and order.[11]

This involvement by the justices in the successful effort to create "institutional unanimity" took place between July 10 and July 23, 1974! The justices and their clerks worked throughout the week and on weekends in Washington and elsewhere—Douglas in Goose Prairie, Washington, and Brennan in Nantucket, Massachusetts—to write, review, and modify drafts in portions of the opinion. Burger's peers placed extreme pressure on him to circulate his drafts of the various sections of the *Nixon* opinion.

Indeed, Burger wrote to his colleagues on July 10 that he would "not await a complete draft but will send sections as they are ready." He ended his note by writing what turned out to be an understated truth: "The enclosed material is not intended to be final and I will welcome—indeed I invite—your suggestions." (Burger handwrote "More later!" on the letter.)[12] (See exhibit 7.2.)

Exhibit 7.2
Chief Justice Burger's Memorandum to the Conference of July 10, 1974

Supreme Court of the United States
Washington, D. C. 20543

CHAMBERS OF
THE CHIEF JUSTICE

July 10, 1974

Re: 73-1766 - U. S. v. Nixon
73-1834 - Nixon v. U. S.

MEMORANDUM TO THE CONFERENCE:

As I stated at the Conference yesterday I will not await a complete draft but will send sections as they are ready.

The enclosed material is not intended to be final, and I will welcome -- indeed I invite -- your suggestions.

Regards,

More later!

On July 11, 1974, Burger sent two additional sections to his brethren; they were on justiciability and Rule 17c. At the July 9 Conference Session, the justices were in general agreement on each of these issues. The next phase, opinion writing, was complex, critical, and sensitive. Poorly crafted opinions written by justices have led to breakdowns of majorities, vote switches to the point that dissents become majority or plurality opinions of the Court (or vice versa), multiple opinions in a case, and so forth. The justices were obviously aware of these possibilities and all were mindful of counsel to the special prosecutor Lacovara's plea in the final moments of oral argument that the Court provide the president and the country with a "definitive," that is, a unanimous judgment against the president.[13]

A review of the Brennan and Douglas docket sheets and notes on the litigation reveals the following pattern of judicial interaction in the creation of *U.S. v. Nixon* opinion. (See exhibit 7.3.)

Clearly Burger was initially involved in the drafting of each segment of *U.S. v. Nixon*. Equally clear is the fact that his colleagues, in almost every segment of the opinion, either preceded him in the drafting of the section or substantively modified the language and direction that Burger had taken. The reason: Burger's work was extremely poor and the others were extremely concerned about producing an embarrassing opinion for the Court in the *Nixon* litigation. Not until July 20, barely four days before the judgment and order of the Court were announced, was a complete draft circulated by the chief. It was, however, not an opinion written by him.

THE FACTS

On July 11, Burger wrote a memo to his colleagues:

> I have received various memos in response to preliminary and partial sections circulated. . . . I think it is unrealistic to consider a Monday, July 15, announcement. The case is too important to 'rush' unduly although it is in fact receiving priority treatment.

As expressed in that memo, although he felt that "we could meet an end-of-the-week announcement, i.e., July 19 or thereabouts,"[14] the unabated flow of memos from Burger's colleagues pushed the date of Court announcement back to July 24. Indeed, so hectic were the intracourt memos on the Burger drafts in *Nixon* that on July 15 he wrote, "My effort to accommodate everyone by sending out 'first drafts' is not working out. I do not contemplate sending out any more material until it is *ready*" (Burger's emphasis).[15]

Revision of the circulated Burger drafts included his "fact"

Exhibit 7.3
Work Flow: *U.S. v. Nixon,* July 10 to July 23, 1974

Area	Drafters	Responses
I. Facts	WEB, 7/10	HAB draft
		WJB to WEB, 7/12: HAB draft is excellent.
		PS to WEB, 7/12: HAB draft is good
		TM to WEB, 7/15: HAB draft is OK
II. Appealability	WOD, 7/5	PS, 7/8 & 11, supports w/ modifications
(Jurisdiction)	WEB, 7/10	
		LP, 7/11, supports Stewart modification
		WOD, 7/11, supports Stewart modification
		TM, 7/15, supports Stewart modification
III. Justiciability	WOD, 7/5	WJB modification of WOD, 7/10
(Intra-branch dispute)		
	WEB, 7/10	LP, 7/11, supports Stewart modification
		WOD, 7/11, supports Stewart modification
		TM, 7/15, supports Stewart modification

Exhibit 7.3—*Continued*

Area	Drafters	Responses
IV. Applicability of Rule 17c	WJB, 7/10	WOD, 7/11, likes it
	LP, 7/8	
	LP, 7/12	WJB, 7/15: supports LP rewrite
	WEB, 7/10	WOD, 7/12: cannot support Burger draft
		BW, 7/12 offers to draft subsitute to WEB draft
		PS, 7/12; supports Brennan's or Burger's drafts
	BW, 7/13	WJB, 7/15: supports BW version
		TM, 7/15: supports White draft
		WOD, 7/15: supports White draft
		(BW draft of 7/13 incorporated into the final opinion)
V. Executive Privilege	LP, 7/8	
	WOD, 7/5	
	WEB, 7/15 & 17	PS, 7/17, offers to draft substitute
		TM, 7/18 supports Stewart
		BW, 7/18, supports Stewart
	PS, 7/17	TM, 7/18, likes Stewart version

segment, the introductory portion of the opinion. Justice Douglas's law clerk in a July 10 memo indicated that there were "several factual inaccuracies (or at least ambiguities) in the statement of facts."[16] (Douglas, on July 11, wrote the chief a short note enumerating the errors.) On July 12 Burger received a memo from his close friend, Harry Blackmun. Since Burger had asked for recommendations and suggestions, Blackmun wrote, "Accordingly, I take the liberty of suggesting herewith a revised statement of facts and submit it to you for your consideration." Given his concern about the impact of this suggested revision on his friend from Minnesota, Blackmun quickly added, "Please believe me when I say that I do this in a spirit of cooperation and not of criticism. I am fully aware of the pressures that presently beset all of us."[17]

Burger also received notes from Brennan and Stewart that same day, and from Marshall on July 15, supporting the Blackmun version of the Statement of Facts. Blackmun's draft was subsequently included in the final Statement of Facts in *U.S. v. Nixon*.

APPEALABILITY: DID THE SUPREME COURT HAVE JURISDICTION TO HEAR *U.S. V. NIXON*?

Douglas's clerk indicated to his boss that "Burger's section on jurisdiction basically tracks very closely the appealability portion of the draft you initially circulated, although the phrasing is changed (often for the worse) in many instances."[18] (The justices had unanimously agreed on July 9 that the case could be appealed, and, a day later, Burger had circulated his draft on appealability.) Paralleling the comments of the law clerks, Justices Stewart and Powell, on July 11, wrote "with all due respect," urging the chief to incorporate Douglas's draft "into the Court opinion."[19] Douglas himself wrote Burger a note on July 11: "Stewart's [and Powell's] proposal meets with my approval and it might be more acceptable to the Brethren than the early preliminary draft which you circulated."[20] On July 17 Marshall told Burger that he too supported Stewart's suggestion that Douglas's comments be incorporated into the final draft.[21] Douglas's views were made the basis of the appealability section of the Opinion.

INTRA-BRANCH DISPUTE AND THE ISSUE OF JUSTICIABILITY

On July 10 Brennan sent Burger a draft of the justiciability segment. Brennan was very concerned about Burger's attitude about being bombarded with drafts of various segments by most of the justices. After noting that his draft "tracks your oral analysis yesterday [at the conference] of the issue," he wrote to the chief:

> Needless to say insofar as its incorporation, or any part of it, furthers your preparation of the opinion I freely deed it to you in fee simple absolute. I don't think I presume in saying that that is also the thought of the Brethren who have sent you memos on this and other issues. I think Lewis, Potter and Bill Douglas (I borrowed some of the attached from Bill's memo) have written out some particularly persuasive views.[22]

Brennan wrote on his copy of the draft that it was "agreed to by BRW, PS & WJB but not circulated pending Chief's revised section."[23]

Essentially the Brennan draft—supported by Stewart (who could "equally cheerfully" support the chief's version) and White,[24] by Douglas on July 11 and 12 (after he read Burger's draft), and, on July 17, by Marshall "unreservedly"[25]—rejected the president's "first and broadest contention" that the federal courts were without power to review the claim of privilege once Nixon asserted it. Balancing the president's second argument that, as a matter of constitutional law, "the (generalized) privilege he has asserted must prevail over the subpoena *duces tecum* in this case" against the need "for disclosure to demands demonstrably material to a criminal prosecution," Brennan wrote that Nixon "may be ordered . . . to produce the requested materials."[26]

Burger's July 11 version was left largely unchanged in the final opinion and took aim at Nixon's intra-branch dispute argument in noting jurisdiction. It was a narrower statement than the Brennan version and, by and large, was the one left in the final version of *U.S. v. Nixon*.[27]

SATISFYING THE REQUIREMENTS OF RULE 17C

Burger, reflecting the vote in Conference, decided that the Supreme Court was "unwilling to conclude that the District Court's evaluation of the special prosecutor's showing [of relevancy, specificity, and admissibility] under Rule 17c was clearly erroneous."[28]

Brennan, on July 10, supported by Douglas, on July 11, suggested to Burger that the Rule 17c section include a note indicating that Sirica concluded that Jaworski had satisfied Rule 17c "but also . . . had demonstrated a need sufficiently compelling to rebut the President's privilege." But on July 12, Douglas, taking another long hard view of Brennan's statement, concluded that the "compelling need" language was inappropriate in a situation where a president "discussing crimes to be committed and/or crimes already committed with and/or by him or by his orders stands no higher than the Mafia with respect to those confidences."[29]

In addition, Justices Powell and White sent separate draft versions of a Rule 17c segment to their colleagues. Powell's, sent on July 12, tried to develop a Rule 17c interpretation that all could accept regarding the "standard to be met in overcoming the privilege." He reminded the chief that "some of us emphasized that a President of the United States . . . must be entitled to a higher level of protection against disclosures than a citizen possessing no privilege who is charged with crime or who may be a witness in a criminal case." Powell was convinced that the Court should not avoid this important issue and rewrote his earlier draft to underscore the (Sirica) "compelling need" criterion in addition to Rule 17c.[30]

Justice White's circulation, also on July 12 (a revision recirculated a day later),[31] focused on the issue of the relevancy and admissibility of the tapes and was to become the core of the final version's Rule 17c section in *Nixon* announced a few weeks later. (Douglas, on July 12 and 19,[32] Brennan on July 15,[33] Stewart on July 15,[34] and Marshall on July 17[35] all wrote to the chief to state their agreement with the White modification of the Rule 17c segment.) White focused on the president's contentions that Jaworski failed to satisfy the requirements of Rule 17c, and regardless of Jaworski's failure, the subpoenaed materials may be withheld in the president's "absolute discretion pursuant to an executive privilege, which is extended to him by the Constitution and is beyond review by the courts."[36]

For White, the critical question was whether the requirements of Rule 17c had been satisfied. Beyond doubt the special prosecutor had (consistent with Rule 17c) established the relevancy and admissibility of the evidence held by Nixon. "On the basis of the record before us, we find no basis for disturbing this conclusion," White wrote in his draft. Contrary to Powell's 17c proposal, however, the memo did not incorporate the "compelling need" language of the Powell and other Rule 17c drafts. White merely said, addressing the fact that Nixon was a party to the suit, that "appellate review, in deference to a coordinate branch of government, should be particularly meticulous to ensure that the standards of Rule 17c have been correctly applied." White concluded that the Court was "fully persuaded" that Sirica's denial of Nixon's motion to quash was consistent with Rule 17c.[37]

As finally written in the Burger opinion, Part III, Rule 17c, was the White draft. The very deferential language of the Powell draft was not incorporated. Instead, the opinion spoke solely to the value of the standard inherent in Rule 17c itself. Burger's use of a colleague's draft was most dramatically evident in this segment of *U.S. v. Nixon*.

THE SUBSTANTIVE ISSUE: THE QUESTION OF EXECUTIVE PRIVILEGE

Even before Burger circulated, on July 15, his first "very rough draft" (and only to Douglas, who was off to Goose Prairie, Washington),[38] Douglas was writing to the chief that the Court need not "reach the decision of whether [executive privilege] is based on the Constitution."[39] Also on July 15, White wrote to Burger about executive privilege. Though White initially agreed with Powell's earlier memo that the privilege is "rooted in the Constitution," he cautioned, "Shielding a conspiracy in the making or in the process of execution carries the privilege too far."[40]

On July 17, just one week before the final opinion was announced, Burger sent a draft of the "executive privilege" section in "rough form" to his colleagues to "expedite" the Court's "undertaking."[41] It contained a few glaring errors of constitutional law, and Justice Stewart, on the same day, sent him a memo noting these and offering a new Section A. The next day, Brennan and Marshall wrote to Burger indicating that they liked his written draft of the section with the Stewart addition.[42]

Burger had crafted a five-part privilege section. Part A examined the location of the privilege—in common law and statutes and in the Constitution—and focused on the question of reviewability of a claim of privilege. Part B reviewed Nixon's claims of absolute privilege. Burger noted that the president argued that the claim rested on two grounds: Article II, executive powers and the "supremacy of each branch within its own assigned area of constitutional duties,"[43] and the separation of powers doctrine, which, according to the president, provides each coordinate branch independence in its own sphere and this insulates the president from honoring the subpoena request.

Burger rejected the absolutist contention: separation of powers, without more, cannot sustain an absolute, unqualified presidential privilege of immunity. But when a president, wrote Burger, exercises one of his basic enumerated war powers, he is "exercising powers at the *very core* of his constitutional role. The courts have shown the utmost deference to presidential actions in the performance of these core functions" (emphasis added).

When so performing a *core function*, then executive privilege, if employed by the president, has to be accepted by a deferential federal judiciary, Burger maintained—including the U.S. Supreme Court. He added, however, that in *Nixon* the privilege claim was not related to an essential function. Therefore, it could be set aside by the Court. But that caveat did not tame the anger of his brethren: the other justices were extremely angry at this extremely dangerous *core function* notion of the chief's. This view of Burger's scared the brethren for it could be used by a president to argue that privilege was being used in association with such an essential or core function of the executive.

Part C focused on the need to "resolve the competing interests [of the Executive and the Judiciary] in a manner that preserves the essential functions of each." While he acknowledged for the first time a presumptive executive privilege in the Constitution, Burger noted that it could not override the necessity of a subpoena to secure evidence in a pending criminal trial. Parts D and E noted that the trial judge did not commit error in ordering the inspection of materials *in camera*.[44] Burger, however, was arguing that there was a constitutional foundation for the executive privilege concept. "Certain powers and privileges flow from the nature of enumerated powers; the protection of the confidentiality of presidential communications has similar constitutional underpinnings."[45]

For Justices Powell, Marshall, Stewart and Brennan, the chief's *core function* language "implied that a President had an absolute constitutional prerogative over his core functions . . . [and] that was precisely Nixon's claim."[46] For them, the Burger view of presidential core functions and his corollary view that courts had to show "the utmost deference to presidential acts in the performance of Article II core functions," if left unchanged, "could invite future chaos."[47]

The brethren's strategy was to try to convince the Chief that the core functions language had to go. Stewart took the lead in addressing the group's concerns to Burger. Stewart's memo to Burger, a "Dear Chief" letter dated July 17, was sharp. There must be an "unambiguous response" to the president's argument that "he alone has the power to decide the question of privilege and that the Judicial Branch has no role to play." He asked that his draft of a new Section A be considered by his colleagues.[48]

Stewart continued the sharp language in his draft. The judiciary "unreservedly reject the claim" that the president alone, "by a simple assertion of privilege,"[49] has an unreviewable power to decide not to deliver the subpoenaed documents and tapes to the U.S. District Court. "Under the Constitution," Stewart wrote, "it is only the Judicial Branch that is ultimately empowered to determine questions of law." Arguing that no person could be a judge in his or her own case, Stewart wrote that "the existence and scope of presidential privilege is thus a judicial question for the Judicial Branch alone to decide."[50]

On July 18th, Brennan left for Nantucket. Before departing, he, too, wrote a note to the chief in which he said that he agreed "with Potter, that St. Clair's argument, that the President alone has the power to decide the question of privilege, must be dealt with. Potter's suggested way is satisfactory to me."[51]

Also on July 18, an evidently chagrined White wrote to Burger. While not wishing to "complicate a difficult task or to increase your labors," and while not objecting to Stewart's change, White "submit[ted] some comments for the Chief's review. The Court does not have to rely on the 'inherent' Article III judicial authority to deal with the review of presidential privilege in this case." The Constitution already provides

> for the enforcement of the laws, and the Special Prosecutor is enforcing criminal laws passed by congress. The Due Process Clause provides for fair trial, the 6th Amendment provides for compulsory processes for witnesses, and the United States is constitutionally required not to withhold exculpatory materials from defendants in criminal cases. *I doubt, therefore, that we need discover or fashion any inherent powers in the judiciary to overcome an executive privilege which is not expressly provided for but which we also fashion today.*[52] (Emphasis added.)

White concluded by again voicing his concerns about a too broad judicial deference to the use of executive privilege, and referred to the enhanced "compelling need" standard in the Burger draft.

> You are suggesting that there is a dimension to overcoming the privilege beyond the showing of relevance and admissibility. This makes far too much of the general privilege rooted in the need for confidentiality, and it is not my understanding of the conference vote. . . . Relevance and admissibility themselves provide whatever compelling need must be shown.[53]

He closed his note with a threat: "Perhaps none of these matters is of earth shattering importance, but it is likely that I shall write separately if your draft becomes the opinion of the court.[54]

With all these memos coming in, Burger "saw that large accommodations would be necessary."[55] Communicating with his newly found allies Brennan and Douglas, he asked his two senior associates to return to Washington, D.C., to be present for the final deliberations and negotiations. Interestingly, both Brennan and Douglas had begun to work very closely with the chief, and he had come to rely on their advice in the *Nixon* opinion writing process. Burger incorporated the commandatory language of Stewart into Part A of the privilege section, but he did not use White's language (although he had used White's 17c words almost verbatim). White did not write a separate concurring opinion in *Nixon*.

THE SUPREME COURT REACHES, RELUCTANTLY, AGREEMENT ON THE FINAL VERSION OF *U.S. V. NIXON*, JULY 20–24, 1974

On Saturday, July 20, Burger sent two memos to his seven peers. One was attached to the complete draft of the proposed opinion. "This is the first opportunity I (or anyone) have had to see the entire product." While there would "inevitably" be "rough spots," Burger felt that it was unnecessary and unproductive to have a "full scale conference."[56]

The other memo he sent was marked "Personal." It was a note of thanks to his colleagues:

> I have appreciated the helpful suggestions given in this case, some privately and some by general circulation. From the outset we were unanimous on the core issues; . . . I have tried to keep the opinion as straightforward as the basic issues. . . . I have tried to [follow] the restraint and tone of the Burr pattern. The more restrained and even the tone of the opinion the greater will be the force of the holding—or so it seems to me. . . . Whatever problems anyone has can best be resolved by discussing them "across the table." As to each individual's views . . . I will stand ready for any discussion today, Sunday, and thereafter.[57]

Coincidentally, Stewart, Marshall, and White were in the building the same day the printed draft of the Burger proposed opinion was circulated. After reviewing the draft individually, they met with Burger that day to "convey these suggestions. . . . " Stewart was "delegated" to redraft Burger's IV(C)—executive privilege (the "Presumptive Privilege") section.[58]

Stewart, along with White and Marshall visited Burger's office that day to give him their response to his latest draft. The *core functions* language, still in the draft, was what troubled them and the chief justice still refused to remove it from the opinion. Because Stewart saw "that the Chief was growing increasingly adamant," he decided it was better not to continue the debate. Instead, Stewart said, drawing upon the agreement made earlier with the associate justices, he would draft an alternative to Part C and give it to the chief on Monday, July 22. Burger reluctantly agreed.[59]

On Monday, July 22, two days before the opinion was announced from the bench, Stewart sent a memo to the chief, with copies to Douglas, Brennan, Blackmun, and Powell (the four who were not in the building on Saturday). Attached to the memo was a draft of IV(C) that, the justice said,

> embodies the view of Byron, Thurgood and me, and we have submitted it to the Chief Justice this morning. As of now, Byron, Thurgood, and I are prepared to join the proposed opinion, if the recasting of IV(C) is acceptable to the Chief Justice.

Stewart noted in a postscript that "As you will observe, the enclosed draft borrows generously from the draft of the Chief Justice as well as Lewis Powell's earlier memorandum."[60]

The essence of Stewart's amendment was to attempt clarification of the character of executive privilege. Privilege, Stewart wrote, "is fundamental to the operation of government and is inextricably rooted in separation of powers under the Constitution." It is also "constitutionally based," but, given the very strong core value of fair administration of criminal justice, a "balance" must be struck between the "generalized assertion" of privilege and the "demonstrated, specific need for evidence in a pending criminal trial."[61] In that balancing process the federal courts must rule that the generalized privilege must yield to the Rule of Law.

The brethren who reviewed the Stewart modification were delighted with it for it dropped the chief's *core functions* language. Burger's response revealed the character of his intellect. He did not see anything unusual in the Stewart version and wrote to the brethren, that day, that "the two versions can be accommodated and harmonized [and] . . . I will have a new draft of Part 'C' along as soon as possible."[62]

Later that day, a new version appeared that was largely Stewart's language. Dropped from the Segment was Burger's troublesome *core functions* concept. When Brennan queried Burger about the absence of that language, Burger responded very matter-of-factly by noting that core functions was nothing more than " 'the little word discrepancies' between the two versions. . . . [and the chief] had jettisoned [the notion]."[63]

Burger's formal response to his brethren was quickly forthcoming. "I assure you that I will work on it promptly with the hope to accommodate those who wish to get away this week." The chief believed that the two drafts could be "accommodated and harmonized and, indeed, I do not assume it was intended that I cast aside several weeks work and take this circulation as a total substitute."[64]

While Burger was redrafting his opinion (for circulation the following day, Tuesday, July 23), Douglas's law clerk conveyed a message to the justice from one of Justice Brennan's law clerk's:

> Brennan is very much in agreement with the enclosed memo from . . . Stewart regarding [Burger's] latest circulation in the Nixon case. Apparently there are five Justices who are in agreement on the position in the memo from . . . Stewart. Mr. Justice Brennan would like to speak with you about the circulation from [Burger and Stewart].[65]

(That day, one of Douglas's clerks indicated to Douglas that the eighth draft of his opinion would be circulated to Burger that day.)

On Tuesday Lewis Powell sent some Section IV(C) suggestions to his colleagues. At this late date Powell was still urging great deference to the presidential office. "Normally," he wrote, "a president by virtue of his control of the Executive Branch is in a position to determine whether the greater public interest lies in preserving confidentiality with respect to certain evidence or in making it available for the prosecution of an accused person." He also suggested adding the following: "It is the manifest duty of the Courts to vindicate those guarantees and to do so it is essential that all relevant evidence be produced unless inadmissible because of an applicable privilege or for other valid reasons."[66]

A comment on Douglas's copy of Powell's suggestions stated: "Riders prepared by LP and objected to by WOD with vigor—and dropped by LP—WOD"[67] Burger carefully avoided the problem by writing Powell on July 23 that he was accepting them "subject always to the views of the four!"[68] Powell dropped the suggestions.

Years later, in 1987, Powell defended his views on executive privilege. He still maintained that

> "to the extent that the interest in confidentiality pertains to the President's effective exercise of his executive powers, [executive privilege] is constitutionally based" . . . but it is not absolute. In notes I prepared as a basis for discussion at one of our Conferences, I stated that a "general expectation of confidentiality is essential to the effective exercise of Presidential power." And that "the privilege asserted by the President *is* based on the Constitution, Art. II." Justice Douglas had prepared an opinion. If he had filed his, I planned to circulate and file mine. But all of us recognized the utmost importance of unanimity if it possibly could be reached. Douglas, to his credit, was finally persuaded. I think the opinion of the Chief Justice on the privilege issue is sound, and I am happy that it was unanimous."[69] (Powell's emphasis.)

One day before the public announcement, Burger wrote two memos; one was attached to a revised Section IV(c). The other was the second draft of the opinion labelled "Not Proofread." He wrote,

> Immediately on having seven "joins" I will order a full print—obviously with corrections and changes, if any. I suggest that if we need

to meet it should be approximately one-half hour after delivery of this draft. Regards, WEB. P.S. This can be ready by 10:00 AM Wed.[70]

Douglas immediately wrote a memo agreeing with the opinion. "I think the opinion is ready to go and I hope we hand it down tomorrow at 10:00 A.M." He recommended that a "rather full oral announcement should be made" and seconded the call for a conference "today—Tuesday, July 23rd."[71] Burger heard from others, received "joins" from them and, in a final memo, called a conference for 1:30 P.M. "The Bell will be rung at 1:25."[72]

According to the brethren who commented to reporters, the tension was high. Brennan, in the face of criticisms from Douglas and Powell that there were still too many loose ends in the opinion, "made an impassioned plea for unanimity."[73] Brennan's cry seemed to do the trick. They adjourned awaiting the final copy of the opinion from the printer. It came early that evening. The brethren read it and sent their support to the chief. Burger had his unanimous decision for the opinion written by the collective.

UNITED STATES V. NIXON: THE UNANIMOUS OPINION OF THE COURT

On Tuesday, July 24, 1974, at 11:00 A.M., Warren E. Burger, the chief justice of the United States, the first of Nixon's four appointments to the Court, read a thirteen-page summary of the Court's collective opinion in the case of *U.S. v. Nixon*. It summarized the thirty-one page opinion written by the eight justices over the preceding three weeks.

It was a packed Court, full of invited guests (who had their reserved seats due to the logistical work of Justice Rehnquist and his staff), the clerks of the justices, and many dozens of news reporters. It was a solemn place for the Court had tackled an issue and was about to announce a decision that was inextricably connected with the impeachment proceedings that were then taking place in the House Judiciary Committee. Promptly at eleven the brethren entered the Court and, almost immediately, the chief justice, began to read the shortened version of the unanimous opinion.

JURISDICTION OF THE COURT

The first segment of the opinion dealt with the "threshold" question of jurisdiction. The Court concluded that the Sirica order to the president was an appealable order because "the traditional contempt avenue to immediate appeal is peculiarly inappropriate due to the unique setting in which the question arises." *Nixon* was an appropriate exception to the ordinary "finality" requirements. The Court, Burger read, did not have to "require a President of the United States to place himself in the posture of disobeying an order of a court merely to trigger the procedural mechanism for review of the ruling [as that] would be unseemly, and present an unnecessary occasion for constitutional confrontation between two branches of the Government. Similarly, a federal judge should not be placed in the posture of issuing a citation to the President simply in order to invoke review."[74] The appeal from the Sirica order was therefore properly in the Court of Appeals, and the case was "now properly before this Court on the writ of certiorari before judgment."

THE "JUSTICIABILITY" QUESTION

The second critical issue to which the Court responded was the "justiciability" question. The justices had to determine whether or not the "separation of powers" concept precluded the Court from using its power of judicial review to substantively examine the questions raised in the litigation. The counsel for the president had argued that the matter was an intrabranch dispute "between a subordinate and superior officer of the Executive Branch and hence not subject to judicial resolution," that the issue did not present a justiciable "case" or "controversy" "which can be adjudicated in the federal courts."[75]

The Court, Burger read to the packed Courtroom, had to "look behind names that symbolize the parties to determine whether a justiciable case or controversy is present." The starting point for the brethren was a pending criminal proceeding in a federal court, "brought in the name of the United States as sovereign." Congress has delegated power to the attorney general to enforce the nation's criminal and civil laws, and the attorney general "has delegated the authority to represent the United States in these particular matters to a special prosecutor with unique authority and tenure." Prosecutor Jaworski's use of the discretionary powers given to him by the attorney general, and not abrogated by him, included "the power to contest the invocation of executive privilege in the process of seeking evidence deemed relevant to the performance of these specially delegated duties."[76] The clash that arose between the special prosecutor and the president is, in one sense, a typical justiciable controversy heard by the federal courts. In *Nixon*, there is "that concrete adverseness" that must be present for the Court to hear a case on the merits. "In light of the uniqueness of the setting in which the conflict arises, the fact that both parties are officers of the Executive Branch cannot be viewed as a barrier of justiciability," Burger concluded.

WERE THE REQUIREMENTS OF RULE 17C SATISFIED BY JAWORSKI?

After noting jurisdiction and stating that Nixon was a justiciable controversy, that is, one capable of resolution by the federal judiciary, Burger then addressed the validity of the issuance of the subpoena to the president under Rule 17c of the Federal Rules of Criminal Procedure. The President's counsel had challenged the validity of the subpoena on the grounds that the special prosecutor's office had failed to satisfy the requirements, in Rule 17c of the Federal Rules of Criminal Procedure, that govern the issuance of such subpoenas *duces tecum* in federal criminal proceedings.[77]

Was the request of the president that he produce the tapes "unreasonable or oppressive"? That was the primary question examined by the Court. In answering the question, they used the four Rule 17c guidelines formulated in the case of *U.S. v. Iozia*,[78] announced in a federal district court in 1952. Jaworski had the burden of showing that (1) the documents in Nixon's possession were evidentiary and relevant, (2) they were not otherwise procurable reasonably in advance of the trial by the exercise of "pure diligence," (3) Jaworski could not "properly prepare for trial" with the production of the tapes in the president's possession and that the failure to obtain the tapes would tend to unreasonably delay the trial, and (4) Jaworski's request was a good faith one and not a "fishing expedition."

Burger read on that in order to make his showing, Jaworski had to "clear three hurdles: relevancy, admissibility, and specificity." After reviewing the record before them, the justices concluded that Jaworski had made such a requisite showing and had met the burden placed on him by the statute and the judicial gloss of the Rule. The Court adjudged that it was "unwilling to conclude that the District court erred in the evaluation of [Jaworski's] showing under Rule 17c."[79] Jaworski had "made a sufficient showing to justify a subpoena for production *before trial*. The subpoenaed materials are not available from any other source, and their examination and processing should not await trial in the circumstances shown."

THE CONSTITUTIONAL ISSUE: THE CLAIM OF EXECUTIVE PRIVILEGE

Having laid the basis for judicial review, the reader of the opinion then went on to discuss the most controversial portion of the decision in *U.S. v. Nixon*: whether the president had an inherent constitutional executive privilege or whether it was a prerogative that was not constitutionally based. The president had asked the Court to quash the subpoena because the separation of powers concept "precludes the judicial review of a President's claim of privilege."[80] His counsel had also argued, should the absolute claim argument fail, that the Court "should hold as a matter of constitutional law that the privilege prevails over the subpoena *duces tecum*."

The Court immediately reaffirmed the notion, first presented in *Marbury v. Madison*, that on the issue of interpreting the Constitution, it is "emphatically the province and the duty" of this Court 'to say what the law is' with respect to the claim of privilege presented in this case."[81]

Reviewing the presidential claim, the Court noted two arguments in support of an *absolute* executive privilege. The first claim was that privilege was constitutionally derived from Article II powers of the president because of the need to retain confidentiality of communications in order to get the best advice possible from presidential staff. The second Nixon claim rests on his assertion that the separation of powers doctrine "insulates a president from a judicial subpoena in an ongoing criminal prosecution, and thereby protects confidential presidential communications."[82]

However, the Court reasoned, these claims, *"without more,"* can "sustain" the presidential argument for an "absolute, unqualified presidential privilege from judicial process under all circumstances."[83] There was nothing but a general, "broad, undifferentiated claim of public interest." Absent "a claim of need to protect military, diplomatic or sensitive national security secrets," the brethren could not accept the argument for privilege as against the perceived need of the prosecutor for the information that was needed for a pending criminal trial. The Court rejected the presidential notion of an absolute privilege because it "would upset the constitutional balance of a 'workable government' and gravely impair the role of the courts under Article III."[84]

The next segment of this part of the *Nixon* opinion dealt with the roots of executive privilege. Did the privilege have its existence in common law or was it a part of the constitutional law? This portion of *Nixon* was, from the justices' own perceptions (as conveyed in their memos to the conference) as well as from the reaction of scholars, the most controversial part of the opinion.

The conservative interpretivists, led in conference by Burger and Powell, won the day by interpreting the constitutional framework in such a manner as to provide a constitutional basis for executive privilege. The Court did admit that no prior cases in the Court extended a high degree of deference to the president's "generalized interest" in the privilege protection. Indeed, Burger read, "nowhere in the Constitution . . . is there any explicit reference to a privilege of confidentiality." However, accepting the value of confidentiality, the court stated that consideration was "justifying a presumptive privilege for presidential communications. The privilege is fundamental to the operation of government and inextricably rooted in the separation of powers under the Constitution. . . . [and] to the extent this interest [in confidentiality] relates to the effective discharge of a President's powers, it is constitutionally based."[85]

With these words, the Court created a "general constitutional privilege of confidentiality of presidential communications."[86] Although it was not an absolute privilege,[87] nevertheless it was a new constitutional law—but it was new constitutional law without any "intent" foundations in the opinion.

The reading of the opinion then reached its conclusion. Having disposed of the jurisdictional and constitutional questions, the Court directed Federal District Court Judge Sirica to continue with the implementation of the subpoena. The tapes were to be transmitted to Sirica's chambers for an *in camera* inspection by the federal judge. Sirica, however, was instructed by the Court, because of the public interest and because of the fact that the president was no ordinary individual,[88] to "accord to presidential records that high degree of deference . . . [and] to afford presidential confidentiality the greatest protection consistent with the fair administration of justice."[89] After the *in camera* inspection, Sirica was to turn over the materially relevant data to Jaworski; all other material "is to be restored to its privileged status and should be returned under seal to its lawful custodian."[90] Burger concluded his reading of the opinion; the Court had concluded its work in the *Nixon* case.[91]

UNITED STATES V. NIXON: AN OPINION BY COMMITTEE

As the chapters have presented and as Schwartz has observed, there was, in *Nixon*, the "absence of one strong hand that has molded the outstanding opinions in our legal history."[92] Instead, because of the stubborness and ineptitude of the chief justice, it was an opinion literally written by six of the eight men who sat on the Court, who participated in the debates surrounding the case, and who had to work around the original drafts prepared by Burger.[93] It was, to say the least, an exasperating experience for the brethren.

Nixon's response was interesting. Through his counsel, James

D. St. Clair, the attorney who valiantly argued the president's case in the court, Nixon issued a statement which said, in part:

> While I am, of course, disappointed in the result, I respect and accept the court's decision, and I have instructed Mr. St. Clair to take whatever measures are necessary to comply with that decision in all respects. For the future it will be essential that the special circumstances of this case not be permitted to cloud the right of Presidents to maintain the basic confidentiality without which this office cannot function. I was gratified, therefore, to note that the court reaffirmed the principle of executive privilege, the principle I had sought to maintain. By complying fully with the court's ruling in this case, I hope and trust that I will contribute to strengthening rather than weakening this principle for the future, so that this will prove to be not the precedent that destroyed the principle but the action that preserved it.[94]

Nixon was an opinion that was initially applauded by millions for it forced the president to provide Sirica with the requested tapes. A major constitutional crisis ended shortly after the Court handed down its opinion. Justice Brennan's argument that the Court had to act quickly in order to have the society at large come to closure on the rending of the community's ethical fabric was accepted and, for the most part, he was proved correct.

A potential confrontation between the Congress and the president and between the president and the Court was avoided. The president turned the tapes over to the federal judge and observed, as noted above, that he was pleased with the Court's adoption of the presidential position that executive privilege was constitutionally based. By August 8, 1974, Nixon was out of the White House and, although his pardon by President Jerry Ford caused a major stir,[95] within six months Richard M. Nixon was in retirement and, for the moment, off the front pages.

However, *United States v. Nixon* was an opinion that was, because of a number of factors, seriously flawed. (Justice Potter Stewart, it has been written, "told his clerks that the Chief's initial draft of the decision would have got a grade of D in law school. It had been raised to a B"[96] by the collective efforts of the other seven associate justices.)

At the core of the criticism of the opinion was the Court's

treatment of the separation of powers and executive privilege concepts. While claiming to act as "judicial interpretivists" in the case, the opinion, as well as the debates, is strikingly barren of any careful examination of the intent of the framers regarding these concepts.

NOTES

1. Memo to the Conference (MTTC), WOD P, Box 1659, Library of Congress, Washington, D.C.
2. Ibid.
3. Docket Book, 1973 Term, Conference Notes, July 9, 1974, Brennan Papers, Boxes 329 and 423, LC. See also Douglas Papers, Box 1627 (Docket Book, 1937 Term), LC, Washington, D.C.
4. Ibid.
5. Ibid.
6. *Cooper v. Aaron* 358 *U.S.* 1 (1958) was a school segregation case that pitted state authority (Arkansas) versus the authority of the national government in the form of federal court orders that had been disobeyed by state officials. It was a critical moment in America's political, social and legal history and the justices, in their unanimous opinion reaffirming the supremacy of the national government, had each of their names affixed to the opinion (as co-authors). See Howard Ball and Philip Cooper, *Of Power and Right* (New York: Oxford University Press, 1991), chapter eight, for a detailed account of this period of history.
7. Justice Brennan, quoted in Jeffrey T. Leeds, "A Life on the Court," *New York Times Sunday Magazine*, October 1986, p. 75.
8. Bernard Schwartz, ed., *Unpublished Opinions of the Burger Court* (New York: Oxford University Press, 1988), p. 276, quoting an unidentified justice who participated in the *Nixon* deliberations.
9. Warren quoted in Ibid., p. 152.
10. Earl Warren, "Richard M. Nixon," *Esquire Magazine*, April 1975.
11. Note, Brennan papers, Box 329, LC, Washington, D.C.
12. MTTC, July 10, 1974, Brennan Papers, Box 329, LC.
13. Lacovara (Special Prosecutor) oral argument before U.S. Supreme Court, in Westin and Friedman, *Nixon*, p. 594.
14. MTTC, July 11, 1974, Douglas Papers, Box 1659, LC, Washington, D.C.
15. MTTC, July 15, 1974, Douglas Papers, Box 1659, LC, Washington, D.C.

16. Memo, DK to WOD, July 10, 1974, Douglas Papers, Box 1659, LC, Washington, D.C.
17. Memo, Blackmun to Burger, July 12, 1974, Brennan Papers, Box 329, LC, Washington, D.C.
18. Memo, law clerk to Douglas, July 10, 1974, Douglas Papers, Box 1659, LC, Washington, D.C.
19. Ibid.
20. Douglas to Burger, July 11, 1974, Douglas Papers, Box 1659, LC, Washington, D.C.
21. Marshall to Burger, July 17, 1974, Douglas Papers, Box 1659, LC, Washington, D.C.
22. Brennan to Burger, July 10, 1974, Brennan Papers, Box 329, LC, Washington, D.C.
23. Ibid.
24. Stewart to Burger, July 11, 1974; and White to Burger, July 11, 1974, Douglas Papers, Box 1659, LC, Washington, D.C.
25. Marshall to Burger, July 17, 1974, Douglas Papers, Box 1659, LC.
26. MTTC, July 10, 1974, Brennan Papers, Box 329, LC.
27. See 418 *U.S.* 683 (1974).
28. MTTC, July 11, 1974, Brennan Papers, Box 329, LC, Draft p. 5.
29. Brennan to Burger, July 10, 1974, Brennan Papers, Box 329, LC; Douglas to Burger, July 12, 1974, Douglas Papers, Box 1659, LC.
30. Powell to Burger, July 12, 1974, Brennan Papers, Box 329, LC.
31. White to Burger, July 12, 1974, Brennan Papers, Box 329, LC.
32. Douglas to Burger, July 12 & 19, 1974, Douglas Papers, Box 1659, LC.
33. Brennan to Burger, July 15, 1974, Brennan Papers, Box 329, LC.
34. Stewart to Burger, July 15, 1974, Brennan Papers, Box 329, LC.
35. Marshall to Burger, July 17, 1974, Brennan Papers, Box 329, LC.
36. White to Burger, July 12, 1974, Brennan Papers, Box 329, LC.
37. White to Burger, July 12, 1974, Brennan Papers, Box 329, LC.
38. MTTC, July 15, 1974, Douglas Papers, Box 1659, LC.
39. Douglas to Burger, July 13, 1974, WOD P, LC, Box 1659, Washington, D.C.
40. White to Burger, July 15, 1974, Brennan Papers, Box 329, LC.
41. MTTC, July 17, 1974, Brennan Papers, Box 329, LC.
42. Ibid.
43. Ibid.
44. Ibid.
45. Ibid.

46. Robert Woodward and Scott Armstrong, *The Brethren: Inside the Supreme Court* (New York: Simon and Schuster, 1979), p. 330.

47. Ibid. "The Court could find itself with years of work defining what was and wasn't a core function."

48. Stewart to Burger, July 17, 1974, Brennan Papers, Box 329, LC. Stewart pointed out that Burger probably "completely misinterpreted" the St. Clair brief and oral argument when Burger wrote: "Although the President's counsel asserts that the privilege of confidentiality of presidential communications is absolute he does not challenge the authority of this court to interpret the law" (p. 3). Brennan noted another seeming error in the Burger draft when Burger wrote: "The right of privacy of every citizen to the confidentiality of his conversations, private papers and records has been accorded a high place in our concept of liberty *although it is not expressed in the Constitution,*" (p. 7). Brennan had circled the underlined words and had written in the margin, "4th Amendment?"

49. Ibid.

50. Ibid.

51. Memo, Brennan to Burger, July 17, 1974, WJBP, LC, Box 329, LC, Washington, D.C.

52. White to Burger, July 18, 1974, Brennan Papers, Box 329, LC.

53. Ibid.

54. Ibid.

55. Woodward and Armstrong, *Brethren*, p. 332.

56. MTTC, July 20, 1974, Douglas Papers, Box 1659, LC.

57. Ibid.

58. Memo to Douglas, Brennan, Blackmun, Powell, July 22, 1974, Douglas Papers, Box 1659, LC.

59. Ibid., p. 337.

60. Ibid.

61. Ibid.

62. Ibid., p. 340. Brennan noted that "Burger had not even understood the vast difference between the two approaches." Ibid.

63. Ibid., p. 343.

64. MTTC, July 22, 1974, Douglas Papers, Box 1659, LC.

65. Memo, law clerk to Douglas, July 22, 1974, Douglas Papers, Box 1659, LC.

66. MTTC, July 23, 1974, Douglas Papers, Box 1659, LC.

67. Ibid.

68. Burger to Powell, July 23, 1974, Brennan Papers, Box 329, LC.

69. Letter, Justice Lewis F. Powell, Jr. to Howard Ball, December 3, 1987.

70. Burger to Powell, July 23, 1974, Brennan Papers, Box 329, LC.
71. Douglas to Burger, July 23, 1974, Douglas Papers, Box 1659, LC.
72. MTTC, July 23, 1974, Douglas Papers, Box 1659, LC.
73. Ibid., p. 345. "Everyone had problems with the opinion. . . . But it was a compromise document that was essential both to the Court and to the nation."
74. *U.S. v. Nixon*, 418 *U.S.* 683 (1974).
75. Ibid.
76. Ibid.
77. Rule 17c provides that "A subpoena may also command the person to whom it is directed to produce the books, papers, documents or other objects designated therein. The court on motion made promptly may quash or modify the subpoena if compliance would be *unreasonable or oppressive*. The court may direct that books, papers, documents or objects designated in the subpoena be produced before the court at a time prior to the trial or prior to the time when they are to be offered in evidence and may upon their production permit the books, papers, documents or objects or portions thereof to be inspected by the parties and their attorneys."
78. 13 *F.R.D.* 335 (SD, NY).
79. *U.S. v. Nixon* 418 *U.S.* 683 (1974).
80. Ibid.
81. Ibid.
82. Ibid.
83. Ibid.
84. Ibid.
85. Ibid.
86. Ibid.
87. The Court stated that this new constitutionally derived principle of executive privilege has limits. "The generalized assertion of privilege must yield to the demonstrated, specific need for evidence in a pending criminal trial." Ibid.
88. The Court quoted from *U.S. v. Burr* at this point. "In no cases of this kind would a Court be required to proceed against the President as against an ordinary individual." Marshall, on circuit 25 *Fed Cases* 187, 191 (1807).
89. Ibid.
90. Ibid.
91. The tapes were eventually turned over by the president, and the criminal trial took place in the Fall of 1974. On December 26, 1974 the summations were given and, on January 1, 1975, the 64th day of the trial, the federal jury, after deliberating fifteen hours, found

Haldeman, Ehrlichman, Mitchell guilty of various counts of conspiracy, obstruction of justice, false declarations before the Grand Jury, and perjury. Mardian was found guilty of conspiracy. Parkinson was acquited by the jury.

92. Schwartz, *Unpublished Opinions of the Burger Court*, p. 276.

93. Ibid., p. 277.

94. Quoted in Congressional Quarterly, *Watergate: Chronology of a Crisis* (Washington, D.C.: Congressional Quarterly Press, 1975), p. 719.

95. On September 8, 1974, President Gerald R. Ford granted Richard M. Nixon a full pardon. Saying that Nixon's resignation was "an American tragedy in which we have all played a part," the new chief executive used his "constitutional power to firmly shut and seal this book" because years would have to pass before Nixon could receive a fair trial by jury for his criminal behavior. Critics of the decision felt that Ford had acted prematurely. Quoted in CQ, *Watergate*, p. 787.

96. Woodward and Armstrong, *Brethren*, p. 347.

8

Executive Privilege: The Court's Fashioning of an Inherent Presidential Power

Special Prosecutor Leon Jaworski argued before the justices at the oral argument and in his written briefs that executive privilege was not in the Constitution. It was a common-law privilege at best, he argued, and it should not be elevated to the status and standing of a constitutional principle. His arguments, however, did not prevail in the case. Because a majority of the brethren, especially two Nixon appointees (Chief Justice Burger and Justice Powell), had insisted that the presidency had to have the constitutional prerogative, the St. Clair argument was adopted. As a consequence, the Court unanimously created a new constitutional standard.

THE RELUCTANT JOINERS: DOUGLAS, BRENNAN AND WHITE

Justice William O. Douglas was quite concerned about the direction his colleagues were going with executive privilege. He believed that it was a "travesty to think of the case in terms of executive privilege." As he wrote in a letter to Powell, with a copy to the Conference, he urged the Court to view the privilege in more modest terms because, in his estimate, it was not a "constitutionally based" principle; furthermore, as the requested information involved questions of criminal conspiracy, it was not a true Article II case.

His friend William J. Brennan was just as unsuccessful. Brennan also encouraged his peers to downplay the issue of whether the executive privilege was constitutionally based or was, instead, based on common law. He believed that the issue need not be decided.

So, too, was Justice Byron White unsuccessful. He was, briefly, the most critical of the majority's position that the concept of executive privilege was a constitutionally rooted power of the president. As he wrote to the chief justice on July 22, he was very concerned about the Court fashioning out of whole cloth an inherent constitutional power: "I doubt . . . that we need discover or fashion any inherent powers in the judiciary to overcome an executive privilege which is not expressly provided for but which we also fashion today." The Jaworski, Douglas, Brennan, and White view of the issue—that executive privilege was essentially a question not necessary for the court to "reach"[1]—did not find a majority in the 1974 Supreme Court.

THE MAJORITY'S EXECUTIVE PRIVILEGE OPINION: SOME INHERENT PROBLEMS

Chief Justice Warren Burger, who had dissented in the 1971 *Pentagon Papers* case (in which the federal courts restricted the powers of the president to withhold news from the media by using the legal processes of the federal courts to restrain the press), was earnestly committed to the creation of a constitutionally based executive privilege. Although he was forced to accept modifications in his *Nixon* opinion in order to forge an institutional statement of the Supreme Court, the executive privilege segment he penned was only modestly changed. The chief justice refused to cave in to White's short-lived threat and correctly guessed that Douglas would not have his separate opinion published.

From Chief Justice Burger's perspective, there must not be

any additional weakening of the executive branch by the Court in the *Nixon* litigation. He refused to amend the executive privilege segment to constrict presidential behavior. Not to have the privilege constitutionally based was seen by the chief justice as a weakening of the powers of the Executive Branch and that he refused to cause. And so the court majority, with the silent and reluctant acquiescence of Douglas, Brennan, and White, stood firm and held "for the first time"[2] that the president's claim of executive privilege is "fundamental to the operation of government and inextricably rooted in the separation of powers under the Constitution."[3]

Relying on few judicial precedents, chiefly *U.S. v. Burr* (1807),[4] Burger's opinion lacked any detailed reference to the available historical research on the subject of executive privilege.[5] As noted constitutional law scholar Laurence Tribe wrote, "whatever may be the correct resolution of the historical debate, it is unfortunate that the Court paid it no heed."[6] Certainly Burger did not examine the *intent* of the framers of the Constitution on this question, nor did he refer to any scholarly texts that analyzed the constitutional issue. The executive privilege segment in Nixon is bereft of any such historical intent justification. His dilemma, in addition to the element of time, was that there was absolutely nothing on the convention record about this allegedly constitutionally derived principle.

Had there been an effort to search the constitutional convention debates record, Burger would have found that "executive privilege is mentioned neither in the Constitution nor in the Constitutional debates."[7] (For example, Raoul Berger's book on the subject concludes that Nixon's claim that the president had the constitutional authority to withhold information from the Congress or the federal courts simply is not based on the historical record.[8])

The Rule of Law calls for appropriate information, relevant and admissible, in order for justice to be administered fairly. The president cannot, given the clear intent of the framers, unilaterally refuse to provide information that has been correctly requested by coordinate branches of the national government. Article II, as written in 1787, did not contain the inherent power of executive privilege.[9]

The powers of the executive were carefully enumerated by James Madison and others. "Certain powers must be given to the President," Madison wrote, but that power "should be confined and defined."[10] Given these views of the Constitution's framers, it is "incongruous to think they would extend the executive power beyond the confined and defined execution of the laws."[11]

DEFENDING THE POWERS OF THE PRESIDENCY

Burger (for the Court majority), though, was very interested in invoking the concept of executive privilege "to justify withholding evidence and other communicative materials from the legislative and judicial branches."[12] As his earlier dissent from the per curiam order of the Court in the *Pentagon Papers* opinion indicated,[13] the chief justice was clearly concerned about maintaining a broad-based power of the president to withhold information from the media, Congress, and the courts. "The imperative of a free and unfettered press comes into collision with another imperative, the effective functioning of a complex modern government and specifically the effective exercise of certain constitutional powers of the Executive."[14]

Burger's views were philosophically similar to the views of the associate justice on the bench who recused himself from participation and discussion of the *Nixon* case, William H. Rehnquist. In 1971, then-Assistant Attorney General William Rehnquist told a Senate Committee that while the "President's authority to withhold information is not an unbridled one, it necessarily requires the exercise of his judgment [on whether disclosure] would be harmful to the national interest."[15]

Until the 1974 judicial creation of the constitutionally based executive privilege claim made in *Nixon*, presidential claims of that "inherent right to withhold have been rare and the instances of congressional acquiescence have been infrequent."[16] The Burger language in *Nixon*, however, had immediate precedential impact. Burger, in the opinion, correctly and ironically noted that

> no case of the Court . . . has extended this high degree of [judicial] deference to a President's generalized interest in confidentiality. No-

where in the constitution . . . is there any explicit reference to a privilege of confidentiality, yet to the extent this interest relates to the effective discharge of a President's powers, it is constitutionally based.[17]

In *U.S. v. Nixon* the Supreme Court gave its "imprimatur to this executive right to withhold certain information and accorded it constitutional dimension."[18] In a dramatic example of interpretive judicial review, the Court majority in *Nixon* in effect created an inherent constitutional presidential prerogative.

The Supreme Court itself after *Nixon*, in cases such as *Nixon v. Fitzgerald* [1979],[19] *Snepp v. U.S.* [1980],[20] *Haig v. Agee* [1981],[21] and *Weinberger v. Catholic Action of Hawaii* [1981][22] moved to expand presidential powers and prerogatives. It was as if the justices, after *U.S. v. U.S. District Court* [1972][23] and the *U.S. v. Nixon* litigation, felt compelled to show an enhanced deference to the executive branch.

WARREN E. BURGER: A WEAK CHIEF MADE WRITING THE *NIXON* OPINION EXTREMELY PROBLEMATICAL FOR THE BRETHREN

One of the major liabilities the brethren had to confront daily was the intellectual weakness of their chief, Warren Burger. During the many stressful weeks, as the justices groped for the right legal and political solution to the riddle of *Nixon*, they always seemed to run into some Burger factual error, some legal ommission or misinterpretation of precedent.

For example, in the draft Burger sent to the brethren on July 10, he wrote the following about the concept of judicial review:

Like the power of judicial review first announced by this Court under the authority of Article III in *Marbury*, certain powers and privileges from the nature of enumerated powers, the protection of the confidentiality of presidential communication has similar constitutional underpinnings.[24]

Justice Byron White vigorously objected to Burger's erroneous view of judicial review[25] (as did other brethren), but White wrote the following to the chief:

Because I am one of those who thinks that the Constitution on its face provides for judicial review, especially if construed in the light of what those who drafted and said at the time or later, I always wince when it is inferred that the Court created the power or even when it is said that the "power of judicial review [was] first announced in *Marbury v. Madison*." See page four of your draft. But perhaps this is only personal idiosyncrasy.[26]

While the changes did occur after a justice complained to the chief, it was an understandably embarrassing set of circumstances. "To avoid making the rebuff of the chief justice even harsher than it was, the other justices used the Burger draft language as much as possible."[27] Schwartz concluded that the final opinion was "weaker than it would have been had it been authored solely by one of the other justices or even had the sections been the work only of those who redrafted them, without their having to incorporate as much as possible of the original Burger sections."[28] Clearly, Chief Justice Burger was, for a number of reasons (his views about the powers of the presidency and his lack of legal acumen), a heavy burden the other associate justices had to bear while trying to resolve the legal questions associated with *Nixon*.

U.S. V. NIXON: THE CONSEQUENCES

Nixon's reaction to the Court's judgment in his litigation was interesting and, in a sense, perfectly understandable. "I was gratified," he said immediately after reviewing the opinion with his counsel on July 24, "to note that the Court reaffirmed both the validity and the importance of the principle of executive privilege, the principle I had sought to maintain."[29] The Court reaffirmed the president's view, but at a dangerous cost.

The ramification of the newly established inherent constitutional executive privilege created by the brethren was the creation of an extremely "nebulous," boundless description of executive power.[30] By creating the constitutional basis for executive privilege, the Court made it almost impossible for public officials to receive information from the executive branch.

In developing its institutional response to the serious constitutional questions raised in *U.S. v. Nixon*, the Court directed its attention to the concept of separation of powers. Although there was serious disagreement among the justices regarding executive privilege, there was unanimity regarding the role of the federal judiciary in defining the parameters of political system. For the eight jurists, the Supreme Court was, as Potter Stewart wrote in the drafting of *Nixon*, the "ultimate interpreter" of the Constitution.

The Supreme Court rejected the president's mechanical assertion that the separation of powers concept deliberately created insulated, fragmented centers of countervailing power immune from review by the coordinate branches.[31] It concluded that—given the presence of a concrete case or controversy—the concept of separation of powers did not preclude judicial review of the presidential claim of privilege and immunity. Contrary to St. Clair's argument on behalf of the president that Nixon was the sole interpreter of the Article II powers, the Supreme Court reaffirmed its interpretive responsibility, consistent with Article III, to say what the law means (*Marbury v. Madison*, 1803).[32] As Justice Powell wrote in his July 6 draft, judicial review by the Supreme Court defines the "contours" of the doctrine of separation of powers, including the definition and use of the executive privilege concept.

Once the Court began to define the contours of the concept of separation of powers in *U.S. v. Nixon*, however, the Court majority showed unusual deference to a coordinate branch. This deference led to the decision by the brethren on the question of executive privilege. In so acting, five justices set aside the pleas of three of their colleagues (Brennan, Douglas, and White), who thought it unnecessary and unwise to decide the controversial question regarding the nature and the source of the executive privilege: presidential prerogative. More than likely they ran out of time and, probably, energy in their efforts to persuade the others that the Court should not be strengthening the presidency through the judicial creation of the inherent power of executive privilege.

Alan F. Westin has written that *U.S. v. Nixon* was "one of the most predictable rulings in the history of American constitutional law. The political situation was not only hospitable to a ruling against the President but almost irresistibly pressing for it."[33] It was manifestly clear, from the evidence in the justices' files, that the justices were aware of that reality and that they acted with dispatch to fulfill their "duty to end the Watergate crisis."[34]

However credible or noble that action of the Court might have been at the time, the simple truth is that in their commitment to come to judgment quickly, a majority of the justices accepted the arguments of the Nixon attorneys that executive privilege was constitutionally based. It would have been enough for the Court to have ended the crisis; the justices did not have to create a broad constitutional executive privilege.

The precedent, however, has been established. While there was some discussion about executive privilege, there should have been a great deal more reflection and analysis by the judges before the creation of the constitutional privilege. (Between May 31 and July 24, 1974, many strongly held views were expressed—and modified—by the justices, except for the executive privilege principle.) The Court ended the 1974 presidential crisis of Watergate, but by employing interpretive judicial review to define the contours of Article II, it may well have set the stage for future constitutional crises.

NOTES

1. Douglas rarely tried to persuade his colleagues on cases and controversies before the Court. On the issue of executive privilege, however, he was especially active, and his activity was clearly seen in letters written to Powell and Burger, the major Nixon supporters on the issue of executive privilege. In a July 11 letter to Powell, Douglas pleaded with his colleague, because the group was torn between the privilege being grounded in common law or in the Constitution, to "reserve making a decision on it as it is a question not necessary for us to reach on the facts of this case." In a July 12 letter to Burger, Douglas wrote: "I don't think it is necessary to reach the decision of whether [executive privilege] is based on the constitution. The office of the President as I read the Constitution is to executive the laws faithfully. A conspiracy to violate the laws or a conspiracy to protect people who have violated the law cannot be brought under Article 2 of the Constitution. . . . On the basis of the showing so far, conver-

sations relating to law violations are impossible to bring within the scope of Article 2 obligations." In Douglas Papers, Box 1659, LC, Washington, D.C.

2. Jethro Lieberman, *Milestones* (St. Paul: West Publishing Company, 1976), p. 392.

3. *United States v. Nixon*, 418 *U.S.* 683 (1974).

4. *U.S. v. Burr* 25 *Fed Cases* 187 (1807).

5. Anne Y. Shields, "The Supreme Court Under Pressure," *St. Johns Law Review*, 57 (1983): 759.

6. Laurence H. Tribe, *American Constitutional Law* (Mineola: Foundation Press, 1978), p. 202, fn 4.

7. Ibid., p. 202.

8. Berger, *Executive Privilege: A Constitutional Myth* (New York: New American Library, 1974).

9. Ibid.

10. Quoted in Ibid., p. 66.

11. Ibid.

12. Jean M. D'Ovidio, "Executive Privilege," *University of Richmond Law Review*, 18 (1983): 203.

13. See *New York Times v. United States* 403 *U.S.* 713 (1971).

14. Ibid. Burger also joined the dissent of John M. Harlan, II in the Pentagon Papers case. Justice Harlan wrote, in part, that "it is plain to me that the scope of the judicial function in passing upon the activities of the Executive Branch of the Government in the field of foreign affairs is very narrowly restricted. This view is, I think, dictated by the concept of separation of powers upon which our constitutional system rests. . . . It is plain that the scope of [judicial] review must be exceedingly narrow."

15. Quoted in Berger, *Executive Privilege*, p. 9.

16. Ibid.

17. *United States v. Nixon*, 418 *U.S.* 683 (1974).

18. Tribe, *Constitutional Law*, p. 2.

19. 102 *S.Ct.* 2690 (1979).

20. 444 *U.S.* 507 (1980).

21. 453 *U.S.* 280 (1981).

22. 454 *U.S.* 139 (1981).

23. 407 *U.S.* 297 (1972).

24. Memo to the Conference, July 10, 1974, WJBP, LC, Box 329, Washington, D.C.

25. Burger's view was that *Marbury* created the power of judicial review.

26. MTTC, WJBP, LC, Box 329, Washington, D.C.

27. Schwartz, *Unpublished Opinions of the Burger Court* (New York: Oxford University Press, 1988), p. 277.

28. Ibid.

29. Quoted in Congressional Quarterly, *Watergate: Chronology of a Crisis* (Washington, D.C.: Congressional Quarterly Press, 1975), p. 719.

30. Shields, "Supreme Court," p. 760.

31. Tribe, *Constitutional Law*, p. 2.

32. 5 *U.S.* 137 (1803). Chief Justice John Marshall wrote: "It is emphatically the province and duty of the judicial department to say what the law is."

33. In Friedman, *U.S. v. Nixon*, p. xiii.

34. Docket Notes, 1973 Term, Brennan Papers, Box 329, LC.

Selected Bibliography

BOOKS

Abraham, Henry J. *The Judicial Process*. New York: Oxford University Press, 1986.

Ball, Howard. *Courts and Politics*. 2d ed. Englewood Cliffs, NJ: Prentice-Hall, 1987.

———. *No Pledge of Privacy: The Watergate Tapes Litigation*. New York: Kennikat Press, 1977.

———. *The Warren Court's Conceptions of Democracy*. Rutherford, NJ: Fairleigh Dickinson University Press, 1971.

Ball, Howard and Philip Cooper. *Of Power and Right*. New York: Oxford University Press, 1991.

Berger, Raoul. *Government By Judiciary*. Cambridge: Harvard University Press, 1977.

———. *Executive Privilege: A Constitutional Myth*. New York: New American Library, 1974.

———. *Impeachment: The Constitutional Problem*. Cambridge: Harvard University Press, 1971.

Beth, Loren. *Politics, The Constitution and the Supreme Court*. New York: Row, Peterson, 1962.

Bickel, Alexander. *The Least Dangerous Branch: The Supreme Court at the Bar of Politics*. New York: Bobbs-Merrill, 1962.

Blasi, Vincent, ed. *The Burger Court*. New Haven: Yale University Press, 1984.

Bork, Robert. *The Tempting of Justice: The Political Seduction of the Law*. New York: The Free Press, 1989.

Canon, Mark and David O'Brien, eds. *Views from the Bench*. Chatham, NJ: Chatham House, 1985.

Choper, Jesse. *Judicial Review and the National Political Process*. Chicago: University of Chicago Press, 1980.

Clayton, James. *The Making of Justice: The Supreme Court in Action*. New York: E. P. Dutton, 1964.

Clinton, Robert Lowry. *Marbury v. Madison and Judicial Review*. Lawrence, KS: University Press of Kansas, 1989.

Corwin, Edward S. *The Doctrine of Judicial Review*. Princeton: Princeton University Press, 1914.

Cox, Archibald. *The Role of the Supreme Court in American Government*. New York: Oxford University Press, 1976.

Congressional Quarterly. *Watergate: Chronology of a Crisis*. Washington, D.C.: Congressional Quarterly Press, 1975.

Cooper, Philip. *Hard Judicial Choices*. New York: Oxford University Press, 1988.

Douglas, William O. *The Court Years*. New York: Random House, 1980.

Early, Stephen. *Constitutional Courts of the United States*. Totowa, NJ: Littlefield, Adams, 1975.

Ely, John H. *Democracy and Distrust: A Theory of Judicial Review*. Cambridge: Harvard University Press, 1980.

Garvey, John H. and T. Alexander Aleinikoff, eds. *Modern Constitutional Theory: A Reader*. St. Paul: West Publishing Company, 1988.

Harris, Richard. *Decision*. New York: E. P. Dutton, 1971.

Irons, Peter. *Justice at War*. New York: Oxford University Press, 1985.

Jackson, Robert. *The Supreme Court in the American System of Government*. New York: Harper and Row, 1963.

Jaworski, Leon. *The Power and the Right: The Prosecution of Watergate*. New York: Reader's Digest Press, 1976.

Ketcham, Ralph, ed. *The Anti-Federalist Papers and the Constitutional Convention Debates*. New York: New American Library, 1986.

Lasser, William. *The Limits of Judicial Power*. Chapel Hill: University of North Carolina Press, 1988.

Lieberman, Jethro. *Milestones*. St. Paul: West Publishing Co., 1976.

Loss, Richard, ed. *Corwin On The Constitution*. Ithaca, New York: Cornell University Press, 1987.

McCloskey, Paul. *Truth and Untruth: Political Deceit in America*. New York: Simon and Schuster, 1972.

McDonald, Neil. *Novos Ordo Seclorum: The Intellectual Origins of the Constitution*. Lawrence, KS: University Press of Kansas, 1985.

Madison, James, Alexander Hamilton, and John Jay. *The Federalist Papers*, ed. Isaac Kramnick. New York: Penguin Books, 1987.

Mason, Alpheus T. and Donald G. Stephenson, Jr., eds. *American Constitutional Law*. Englewood Cliffs, NJ: Prentice-Hall, 1990.

Murphy, Bruce A. *Fortas: The Rise and Ruin of a Supreme Court Justice*. New York: William Morrow, 1988.

Murphy, Walter F. and C. H. Pritchett, eds. *Courts, Judges, and Politics*. New York: Random House, 1975.

———. *Elements of Judicial Strategy*. Chicago: University of Chicago Press, 1964.

O'Brien, David. *Storm Center: The Supreme Court in American Politics*. New York: W. W. Norton, 1986.

Perry, Michael J. *The Constitution, the Courts, and Human Rights: An Inquiry into the Legitimacy of Constitutional Policymaking by the Judiciary*. New Haven: Yale University Press, 1982.

Rhode, David W. and Harold J. Spaeth. *Supreme Court Decision Making*. San Francisco: Freeman Publishing Co., 1976.

Schlesinger, Arthur M., Jr. *The Imperial Presidency*. Boston: Houghton Mifflin Co., 1973.

Schmidhauser, John R. *Judges and Justices*. Boston: Little, Brown and Co., 1979.

Schwartz, Bernard. *Packing the Courts: The Conservative Campaign to Rewrite the Constitution*. New York: Charles Scribner's Sons, 1988.

———. *The Unpublished Opinions of the Burger Court*. New York: Oxford University Press, 1988.

———. *The Unpublished Opinions of the Warren Court*. New York: Oxford University Press, 1986.

———. *Super Chief: Earl Warren and His Supreme Court*. New York: New York University Press, 1980.

Simon, James F. *Independent Journey: The Life of William O. Douglas*. New York: Harper and Row, 1980.

———. *In His Own Image: The Supreme Court in Richard Nixon's America*. New York: David McKay and Co., 1974.

Sirica, John. *To Set the Record Straight*. New York: W. W. Norton, 1979.

Solberg, Winton U., ed. *The Federal Convention and the Formation of the Union of the American States*. Indianapolis: Bobbs:Merrill, 1958.

Tribe, Laurence H. *God Save This Honorable Court*. New York: Random House, 1985.

———. *American Constitutional Law*. Mineola: Foundation Press, 1978.

Warren, Charles. *The Supreme Court in United States History*. 3 vols. Boston: Little, Brown and Co., 1926.

Wasby, Stephen L. *The Impact of the United States Supreme Court*. Homewood, IL: Dorsey Press, 1970.

Westin, Alan and Leon Friedman, eds. *United States v. Nixon*. New York: Chelsea House, 1975.

White, Theodore. *Breach of Faith: The Fall of Richard Nixon*. New York: Atheneum, 1975.

Witt, Elder. *A Different Justice: Reagan and the Supreme Court*. Washington, D.C.: Congressional Quarterly Press, 1986.

Woodward, Robert and Carl Bernstein. *The Final Days*. New York: Simon and Schuster, 1976.

———. *All the President's Men*. New York: Simon and Schuster, 1974.

Woodward, Robert, and Scott Armstrong. *The Brethren: Inside the Supreme Court*. New York: Simon and Schuster, 1979.

ARTICLES

Ball, Howard. "The Convergence of Constitutional Law and Politics in the Reagan Administration: The Exhumation of the 'Jurisprudence of Original Intent' Doctrine." *Cumberland Law Review* 16 (Fall 1987).

Bickel, Alexander. "Foreword: The Passive Virtues." *Harvard Law Review* 75 (1961).

Brennan, William J. "Inside View of the High Court." *New York Times Sunday Magazine*, October 1963.

Brest, Paul. "The Fundamental Rights Controversy: The Essential Contradictions of Normative Constitutional Scholarship." *Yale Law Journal* 90 (1981).

Casper, Gerhard. "An Essay on Separation of Powers: Some Early Versions and Practices." *William and Mary Law Review* 30 (1989).

Chayes, Abram. "Public Law Litigation and the Burger Court." *Harvard Law Review* 96, no.4 (1986).

Clark, Tom C. "The Internal Operation of the U.S. Supreme Court." *Judicature* 43 (1959).

Corwin, Edward S. "Supreme Court and Unconstitutional Acts of Congress." *Michigan Law Review* 4, no.616 (1906).

Cox, Archibald. "Executive Privilege." *University of Pennsylvania Law Review* 122 no.1383 (1974).

D'Ovidio, Jean M. "Executive Privilege." *University of Richmond Law Review* 18 (1983).

Dahl, Robert. "Decision Making in a Democracy: The Supreme Court as a National Policy Maker." *Journal of Public Law* 6 (1957).

Danielski, David. "The Influence of the Chief Justice in the Decisional Process." Paper Presented at the September 1960 Annual Meeting of the American Political Science Association.

Diggins, John P. "The Judge [Bork] Pleads His Case." *New York Times Book Review*, November 1989.

Freund, Paul A. "Foreword: On Presidential Privilege." *Harvard Law Review* 88 (November 1974).

Genovese, Michael. "Richard M. Nixon and the Politicization of Justice." Paper Presented at the September 1987 American Political Science Association Annual Meeting.

Gunther, Gerald. "Judicial Hegemony and Legislative Autonomy." *UCLA Law Review* 22, no.30 (1974).

Howard, J. Woodford. "On the Fluidity of Judicial Choice." *American Political Science Review* 62 (March 1968).

Katz, Ellis. "Patterns of Compliance with the Schempp Decision." *Journal of Public Law* 14 (1965).

Leeds, Jeffrey T. "A Life on the Court." *New York Times Sunday Magazine*, October 1986.

Mishkin, Paul J. "Great Cases and Soft Law: A Comment on *U.S. v. Nixon*." *UCLA Law Review* 22, no.76 (1974).

Maltz, Earl M. "Murder in the Cathedral: The Supreme Court as Moral Prophet." *University of Toledo Law Review* 8, no.3 (Summer 1983).

Mendelson, Wallace. "Mr. Justice Douglas and Government by Judiciary." *Journal of Politics* 38, no.4 (November 1976).

Nagel, Robert F. "The Legislative Veto, the Constitution and the Courts." *Constitutional Commentaries* 2, no.61 (1986).

Pierce, Richard J. Jr. "*Morrison v. Olson*: Separation of Powers and the Structure of Government." In *1988—The Supreme Court Review*, ed. Philip Kurland, et al. Chicago: University of Chicago Press, 1988.

Powell, Lewis F. "What the Justices are Saying." *American Bar Association Journal* 62 (1981).

Rhode, David. "Policy Goals and Opinion Coalitions in the Supreme Court." *Midwest Journal of Political Science* 26 (May 1972).

Roche, John P. "Judicial Self-Restraint." *American Political Science Review* 49, no.722 (September 1955).

Shields, Anne Y. "The Supreme Court Under Pressure." *St. John's Law Review* 57 (1983).

Strauss, Peter L. "The Place of Agencies in Government: The Separation of Powers and the Fourth Branch." *Columbia Law Review* 84, no.573 (1984).

Totenberg, Nina. "Behind the Marble, Beneath the Robes." *New York Times Sunday Magazine*, March 1975.

Tushnet, Mark. "Following the Rules Laid Down: A Critique of Interpretivism and Neutral Principles." *Harvard Law Review* 96 (1983).

———. "Darkness on the Edge of Town." *Yale Law Journal* 39, no.6 (May 1980).

Warren, Earl. "Richard Nixon." *Esquire*, April 1975.

CASES

Alexander v. Holmes County, Mississippi, 396 *U.S.* 1218 (1969)
Ashwander v. T.V.A., 297 *U.S.* 298 (1936)
Baker v. Carr, 369 *U.S.* 186 (1962)
Brown v. Allen, 344 *U.S.* 443 (1953)
Brown v. Board of Education, 347 *U.S.* 483 (1954)
Colegrove v. Green, 328 *U.S.* 549 (1946)
Cooper v. Aaron, 358 *U.S.* 1 (1958)
Cooper v. Telfair, 4 *Dall* 14 (1800)
Dred Scott v. Sanford, 60 *U.S.* 393 (1857)
Eakin v. Raub, 12 *S&L* 330 (1825)
Eisenstadt v. Baird, 405 *U.S.* 438 (1973)
Ex Parte McCardle, 74 *U.S.* 506 (1869)
Flast v. Cohen, 392 *U.S.* 83 (1968)
Goldwater v. Carter, 62 *L Ed* 2d 428 (1979)
Griswold v. Connecticut, 381 *U.S.* 479 (1965)
Haig v. Agee, 453 *U.S.* 280 (1981)
Hayburn's Case, 2 *Dall* 409 (1792)
Hylton v. United States, 3 *Dall* 171 (1796)
Korematsu v. United States, 323 *U.S.* 214 (1944)
Lloyd Corporation v. Tanner, 407 *U.S.* 551 (1972)
Lochner v. New York, 198 *U.S.* 45 (1905)
Luther v. Borden, 7 *Howard* 1 (1849)
Maybury v. Madison, 1 *Cranch* 137 (1803)
Morrison v. Olson, 108 *S Ct* 2597 (1988)
Myers v. United States, 272 *U.S.* 52 (1926)
Nader v. Bork, 366 *F Supp* 104 (1974)
New York Times v. United States, 403 *U.S.* 713 (1971)
Nixon v. Administrator of General Services, 433 *U.S.* 425 (1975)
Nixon v. Fitzgerald, 102 *S Ct* 2690 (1979)
Nixon v. Sirica, 487 *F 2d* 700 (1977)
Plessy v. Ferguson, 163 *U.S.* 537 (1896)
Reynolds v. Sims, 377 *U.S.* 533 (1964)

Roe v. Wade, 410 *U.S.* 113 (1973)
Schenck v. United States, 249 *U.S.* 47 (1918)
Sierra Club v. Morton, 405 *U.S.* 727 (1972)
Snepp v. United States, 444 *U.S.* 507 (1980)
Tileston v. Ullman, 318 *U.S.* 44 (1943)
United States v. Burr, 25 *Fed Cases* 187 (1807)
United States v. Nixon, 418 *U.S.* 683 (1974)
United States v. U.S. District Court, 407 *U.S* 297 (1972)
Weinberger v. Catholic Action of Hawaii, 454 *U.S.* 139 (1981)
Van Horne's Lessee v. Dorrance, 2 *Dall* 304 (1795)
West Coast Hotel Co. v. Parrish, 300 *U.S.* 379 (1937)
Youngstown Sheet and Tube Company v. Sawyer, 343 *U.S.* 579 (1952)

CONGRESSIONAL HEARINGS

Nomination of Robert H. Bork to Be an Associate Justice of the United States Supreme Court. U.S. Senate, Report of the Committee on the Judiciary, 100 Congress, First Session (1987).
Reorganization of the Federal Judiciary. U.S. Senate, Report on the Committee on the Judiciary, 75 Congress, First Session (1937).

Index

ABOUT THE AUTHOR

HOWARD BALL is Professor of Political Science and Dean of the College of Arts and Sciences at the University of Vermont. He is the author of dozens of political science and law review articles and has authored or co-authored sixteen books on the Supreme Court and the judicial process, including *Compromised Compliance* (co-author) (Greenwood, 1982) and *Judicial Craftsmanship or Fiat* (Greenwood, 1978).